Heart-warming Stories of Love and Miracles

Greetings

This book is fitting for the season and the New Year. The words in the poem on the back cover are particularly moving. This is particularly so when we are faced with so many uncertainties in life: newly emerging diseases, terrorism and so on. VLN has selected this book as a gift to you as it contains so many inspiring & enriching stories. Furthermore, the proceeds from sale of the book go to: "The Love of Vicentica Foundation," a small contribution from VLN to a noble cause. VLN will continue to strive to make such contributions to children around the world. I and my team at VLN wish you all the best in 2011 and all coming years.
Mohan
:):):):)

Thalia Narag Cayetano

Some of the names, places, ages, and other identifying details have been changed to protect the confidentiality of the people in these stories.

Heart-warming Stories of Love and Miracles

Published by Iceni Books™
610 East Delano Street, Suite 104, Tucson, Arizona 85705 U.S.A.
www.icenibooks.com

International Standard Book Number: 1-58736-459-X
Library of Congress Control Number: 2005901528

CONTENTS

CONTENTS

DEDICATION

To God almighty, the source of all grace, the author of love—thank you for making me feel your love and for making it the hallmark of my existence.

To the Blessed Virgin Mary, mother of God, my mother too—thank you for your intercession. Your examples of love, purity, meekness, gentleness, and obedience to God have been my inspiration through the years.

To my husband, Kay, who has always been so understanding and supportive; and to my precious daughter, Avanina, who stirs my heart to love every time I see her little expressions of endearment. Thanks to both of you for appreciating even the little things that I do.

To my mother, who early in my life taught me to love and fear God. I am forever grateful to you for raising me up through stringent discipline that was accompanied by towering love. Thanks for spending some time to write some of your stories and for allowing me to publish them in this book.

You are one of the main reasons this book came about.

To my father, whose quiet demeanor and keen interest in music inspired me to be sensitive to listen to the voice of God in my heart. Thank you for showing us that simple living can also bring happiness.

My heart overflows with love and longing for my brothers and sisters in the Philippines. May you continue to pass on the love that God has given you, and share the knowledge of Him to those who do not know Him.

To Father John Maxwell, the parish priest of St. John the Baptist Catholic Church. Thank you for helping me understand some of the Catholic terms and beliefs.

To all my friends at St. John's multi-cultural choir; my friends at the Bible study group; and to all my fellow Cursillistas. Thank you for your guidance and prayers. May we never get tired of walking alongside each other on the path that leads us home to our heavenly Father.

To all my other friends, co-workers, and relatives—you are God's gifts to me.

To the people of Batanes, my beloved home province, whose examples of simplicity and humility have inspired me to care for the poor and the lowly. May your faith in God be your treasure.

To all of you who are reading this book right at this moment. May your passion to love burn in your hearts anew.

PREFACE

Heart-warming Stories of Love and Miracles is a compilation of true-to-life stories personally experienced or witnessed by me and my mother, JC Narag. A few were told to us by another family member. My mom is a gifted storyteller. She remembers stories from her childhood told her by her highly principled father.

When I was a child, my mom's heartwarming stories never failed to maneuver my heart to love. Later on, I realized that I was becoming like my mom. I, too, have stories to tell. They are stories that can be easily shared by someone who has the passion to love, stories that can be easily understood by someone who has ever loved.

I grew up in a family where love is highly expressed and demonstrated. My seven brothers and sisters have stories to tell about people who sparked their hearts to love, and about some whose hearts they have inspired to love.

Heart-warming Stories of Love and Miracles is published as one of my initial attempts to tell the world that God's extraordinary love and power can be experienced by even the most ordinary, modern-day Christian like me. Experience taught me that when we listen to our hearts in silence, we get to experience the infinite and unconditional love God has for each of us. It is the awareness of His enormous love that gives us the natural inclination to love unconditionally.

After reading this book, may you start thinking of the times when God made His love for you manifest—through a person, an event, a Bible verse, a sermon, a dream, or even a song. I hope you will acknowledge them as phenomena to remind you of the greatness of God's love. If your heart is ignited to love every time you think of these, you, too, have stories to tell.

ABOUT THE AUTHOR

 halia Vicentica N. Cayetano is founder of The Love of Vicentica Foundation. She holds a Bachelor of Arts degree in communications from the University of Santo Tomas, Philippines, and finished her MBA in Project Management from the American Intercontinental University.

Thalia was born and grew up in Basco, Batanes, Philippines. She now lives in California with her husband and daughter. Sharing what she has to the less fortunate gives her immense joy and comfort, so much so that it often offsets the burden of homesickness.

She is currently working on three books: *My Heart Speaks in Silence*, *The Silent Acts of Love*, and the second edition of *Heart-warming Stories of Love and Miracles*. Net proceeds from the sale of this book go directly to The Love of Vicentica Foundation. To learn more about the foundation, please visit www.VicenticaFoundation.org.

About the Contributor

JC Narag has a B.S. degree in education (English) with some M.A. units in psychology from the University of the Philippines. She teaches ethics, psychology, and effective communication in English at Saint Dominic College, Basco, Batanes, Philippines. She was founder and staff adviser of *The Aquinian*, the school paper of the college. She co-chaired the editorial board and contributed to *The Charms of Mt. Iraya and Other Ivatan Stories*. She has been president of a women's group in Batanes for the last thirty years. She was the provincial head of the Philippine Information Agency until she retired.

JC Narag is a mother of eight children, all grown up and with college degrees in the social and behavioral sciences.

Life on earth is a journey to heaven—our final destination. Let us not concentrate too much on reaching the end of the journey by ignoring the beautiful creation around us and the wonderful experiences that can help us reach the end of the tour. With genuine and steadfast love, heaven is never far away. Enjoy the journey!

—Thalia

ONE

Are You Carrying Me, O Lord?

Thalia Narag Cayetano

September 27 to 30, 1995 are the dates in my life that I will never forget. These were my days in Cursillo, a three-day study of Christianity.

For more than a year, a woman named Elsa had been inviting me to join the class. Almost every day, after a church service, she would wait for me in front of the church to woo me into joining the next Cursillo class that her Christian group was sponsoring. Knowing the predictability of her intentions, every time I prepared for church I also made up an excuse not to join the event. Even so, she never gave up.

One day, I got tired of her unending persuasion. I accepted her invitation with the intention to cancel at the last minute.

It was September 27, Wednesday. The Cursillo would start in the evening. My brother and I were having fun with a card game in the living room. I totally forgot about my commitment with Elsa. To my great surprise, she came to pick me up for the Cursillo at seven o'clock. My facial expression clearly revealed my emotions at that time. My pupils moved from side to side as I tried to think of a last-minute excuse.

What am I going to say? Can I tell her I am sick? Can I use the weather as an excuse? But I do not look ill, and oh, it's not even drizzling!

Elsa seemed to know that I was trying to come up with an excuse.

Boldly, I told her, "I can't go with you tonight because I am not prepared. I mean, my stuff is not ready."

"I will wait for you," she replied. "You still have about an hour to prepare." I looked at my brother, hoping that he would rescue me from this big trap by saying he would not let me go, but instead, he nodded his head in approval.

With a heavy heart, I walked to my bedroom and started to pack. The strangest thing was, I was seeing myself doing something that was totally against my will. On our way to the Cursillo house, my soul was full of cynicism regarding the woman who tricked me into joining this class.

Why would I spend my weekend with things and people that are not important to me? I don't think I need this class. I was raised in a Christian home and finished my college in a Catholic university. What else will be new to hear or learn? Let alone for three days?

A few more minutes and we arrived at the Cursillo site. The building was old. I walked around inside and I saw a big room full of small bunk beds. Elsa told me that one of those would be my bed. I looked farther to the end of the room and saw five cubicles with curtain doors. Without me asking, Elsa told me that those would be the shared bathrooms. *This is really a punishment*, I thought. *Do I need to go to such a place to learn about God?* The more I looked around, the more I wanted to go home. Then I decided to go back to the classroom where most of the candidates were. The candidates came from all walks of life—men and women with an age range of eighteen to fifty. When we were introduced, I learned that some were professionals, others were out-of-school youths, and it was whispered to me that three candidates were alcohol-dependents and robbers.

A few minutes before the class, the leaders brought in a lady named Lucy. She was defiantly thwarting anyone who tried to hold her there. I overheard somebody say that she was a drug addict and was pulled from the streets to join the Cursillo. She was cursing and shouting, "I don't need God! I can live without Him! Take me back to the streets!"

Just like me, she wanted to get out of the building, but the leaders would not let us. After signing an agreement, we would not be allowed to leave the facility except for emergencies.

Well, I said to myself, *I will just stay for the experience. Lord, it better be a good one.*

Click. The lights went off. Suddenly, it was total darkness and absolute silence. After a few minutes, we were asked to look at a picture of

Jesus Christ that was glowing in the dark. The moderator started to set our moods to meditation.

I died on the cross so you may live. What have you done in return?

This was the message that I got from my meditation. The message was so resoundingly clear that I could not contain my emotions anymore. All my sins in the past came back to haunt me. I heard God enumerating all the occasions when I had offended Him. I'd thought I was a good child of God, but I was not. Like a movie unfolding before my eyes, God unveiled to me my past and present hurts. At that moment, I felt humility replacing the pride that I'd never realized was there. I started crying out loud until the room was full of wailing sounds. I then realized that it was not just me who was crying.

That was the first night. The meditation was just to help us get ready for the next three days. The moderator instructed us to walk quietly toward the bedroom. I went straight to a bed where my name tag was attached to the frame. Before I closed my eyes, I thanked God for making me humble in an instant. I accepted whatever the facility could offer. Looking at the ceiling from the upper cot of the bunk bed, I whispered, "Dear God, thank you for calling me to join the Cursillo. I have decided to learn more about you."

Every day spent in Cursillo brought me closer to God. The more I knew Him, the more I loved Him. The more I loved Him, the more I needed Him. My ardent thirst for Him grew by the day, and three days of study were not enough. Because

I opened my heart to Him, I began to appreciate the teachings and practices of my religion.

Saturday, September 30, 1995. It was the last day of the Cursillo. I felt dehydrated due to too much crying and unburdening. I also lost some pounds, for I'd lost my appetite to eat for three days. Though the meals were excellently pre-pared, I got less concerned with my physical nourishment as I nurtured my soul with the won-ders of God.

At four p.m., after a short entertainment of songs given by old-time Cursillistas, we started to receive our completion certificates. As I walked toward the stage to get mine, my heart started to pound. I said a prayer in my heart:

"Lord, this certificate will be a constant reminder that for three days in my life, I opened my heart to you com-pletely. I have always been a student and civic leader in school and in the community. This time, I know that you are calling me to be a leader for your cause. Lord, I'll try my best to lead people to you not just by words but by example. I rely on you, though, to lead me to the right direction. In Jesus' name I pray."

The certificate did not look to me like a paper to mark an accomplishment but an invitation to initiate a more important mission. After receiving our certificates, each of us was given a chance to talk about our individual experiences. Everybody was touched by the Holy Spirit. I almost did not recognize Lucy, for her face was bright and peace-ful. Her testimony moved me:

"I am proud to tell everyone that I am a new person. God has cleaned up my heart and so the demon is afraid to touch it. On the second day of the class, my craving for drugs was powerfully replaced by a strong desire to receive God. This desire alone has changed me. I will never allow drugs to enslave me again. I cannot wait to tell people about this experience. I cannot wait to go back to my family and tell them I love them. Do you think they will forgive me?" Lucy cried.

Walking out of the building after the three-day class was my first vulnerable step as a renewed Christian. We were warned that Satan would meet us at the door to lure us to go back to our old sinful ways. I kept that in mind. I focused my thoughts, my emotions, and my senses on the God that I had just experienced in the Cursillo. With God's spirit burning in me, I was joyfully soaring in the air. I could hardly feel my feet on the ground. My family noticed that a more humble, kind, gentle, and loving member of the family came home that night. I went to bed on Saturday night hoping that I would wake up with the same kind of feeling.

The following day, I thanked God that Satan had not taken away the peace and joy that I had had for the past four days. The rain was pouring down heavily. I could not find an umbrella or a raincoat, but the stormy weather did not stop me from walking to the nearest church. Even with the water adding weight to my clothes, my body was light. I stooped to check if my feet were really on the ground. As I looked straight ahead, I saw a woman in her eighties walking toward me. In the rain, I could not believe that she managed to stop just to cast me a beautiful smile. I smiled back and said, "God bless you!"

I suddenly remembered Elsa, the woman who never gave up on inviting me to join the Cursillo. Had I known how wonderful it was to experience God in my heart, I would have yielded to her invitation a long time ago.

I continued walking in the rain, enjoying the splendid feeling that was infusing my whole being. I thought to myself that flying is not only for angels and birds. It is also for people who love too much and put their full trust in God. I laughed out loud and said, "Are you carrying me, O Lord? If you are, I just want to say 'Thank you.'"

A Thought

For many years, God continuously knocked on my door to invite me to discover greater things about Him. I never opened my door to Him. In the person of Elsa, He waited patiently until I finally let Him in.

Prayer

Lord, when you knock on my door, let me not think twice but rush to the door to open it for you. Let me at least give you a chance to place your feet on my doorstep. And once I have accepted you in my life, may I never forget that conversion is not a one-time event but a daily decision to follow you.

TWO

The Little Red Fish

JC Narag

"Tell me again the story of the little red fish," I used to ask my father. So he would sit in his rattan lazy chair and I would sit on a wooden stool. I would position myself in front of him, a little to the left. That way, I could see my Dad's every gesture—his eyes as they squinted, or his long eyelashes that seemed to tremble with excitement at some high points in the story.

Val, my father's neighbor and friend, was a municipal government employee. One weekend, Val and three other friends were coming home from Sabtang in a small rowboat. They expected to reach Uyugan, their home town, in about an hour.

Midway across the channel, the skies turned dark and an alarming wail of a rush of wind pierced their tranquil souls. Soon, angry raindrops filled the little wooden boat and giant waves dashed against it. For more than half an hour, the men tried to row as hard as they could, but the current was so strong that Val felt the boat was being carried away far, far out into the windswept seas. Suddenly, he felt the boat being totally submerged under the churning water. Val never let go of the boat. It was his only hope, his only security.

For a few minutes, the skies cleared a little. Val and only one of his friends were clinging to what was left of the boat. It was now just drifting, its bottom up. One man was floating face down, more dead than alive. The third friend was clinging to a tiny wooden piece dislodged from the boat's side.

Suddenly, a strong gust of wind accompanied by terrifying lashes from the raging waves swiftly disintegrated the boat.

Val was sure now that he was alone. He remembered the short prayers his mother had taught him. "Lord, have mercy on me. Mary, mother of God, pray for me." Then he held onto a small piece of wood and pushed himself mightily, paddling toward Ivana, the closest town.

The sky and the sea began to clear up. Val was on the edge of exhaustion but he persevered with his lonesome journey home. He gave one weary look at the open seas before him, and to his horror, a big black form was moving swiftly toward him. He knew from the tales of old that this was a shark. It opened its jaws and its big, exposed choppers frightened Val so profoundly that he kicked hard and lost his grip on the piece of wood.

He recited his Act of Contrition as he resigned to a "fishy" death.

Just then, he saw a friendly little red fish. It was swimming round and round him, as if trying to protect Val from the shark. The "jaws" was preparing to strike again. But the little red fish positioned itself between Val and the terror of the seas. It sallied forth against the "jaws" each time the latter poised for an attack. To Val's surprise, the shark stopped chasing him and left him alone.

The little red fish went on swimming along-side Val. For many hours, he stood guard for him against any sea animal that was bigger than itself until, finally, Val could see the transparent water kissing the white sand.

A few more meters and Val would reach the shores of Ivana. Feeling powerless from exhaustion and emotional strain, he closed his eyes and back-floated. He felt a sense of security as the setting sun darted its glow into his face.

In a wink, he remembered his friend, the little red fish. He kicked hard and tried to paddle back to a breaststroke position. He swam back some twenty meters to track down his savior. He felt some coral grating under his heels, but the little red fish was nowhere to be found.

Val waded back toward the shore, thanking God for sending him the little red fish as his guide, which, he believed, was his guardian angel.

A Thought

In our toilsome journey to holiness, sometimes we lose track of our real direction and get lost. But if we persevere and seek God with absolute trust and surrender, He gives us the guidance that brings us to the right path.

Prayer

Lord, when I lose the trail that leads me to you, please give me the will and the courage to find it again; lest I'm lost forever.

THREE

The Angel Who Turned the Engine On

Thalia Narag Cayetano

"Mom, I'll be away for a few hours. If I'm not home before the church bells ring for the novena, don't start putting on your worry lines. The angels will surely be with me," I told my mom as I kissed her on the cheek.

"Okay, but try not to deliver a baby again as late as two o'clock in the morning," my mom jokingly said.

"All right," I said with a chuckle.

My mom was referring to an event that had happened a few days back when she and my dad had gone around the town looking for me. She later understood that I had not been an aimless wanderer when I left the house in my Jeep.

That earlier moonless night in the town of Basco, I was on my way home when an old man requested me to give him a ride to his home town, Uyugan, a few miles away. He said he'd missed the last trip of the public transit and knew nobody with whom he could stay for the night in the town proper. I assured him not to worry because I would drive him all the way to his doorstep.

It was already nine o'clock when I got back from Uyugan. In the middle of the unlit streets of Basco, a lady gestured me to halt.

"Please, please, I cannot find a ride. I walked from the hillside to your town to look for a midwife. I already talked to one who is willing to come with me but we don't have a ride and it's too dark to walk to the hillside. My daughter is giving birth any minute now and there's nobody around to help her."

"Come and lead me to the midwife's house," I said without hesitation.

While the three of us were driving to the hillside, the two women started to express their concern that it might have been my first time driving up the hills. I assured them that they needn't worry. I guess I was too excited about helping. I believed my mom when she said that God never forsakes a helpful person.

We stopped in the middle of a narrow, sloping road. It was totally dark, for there was no electricity on that side of the town. In a breath, the two women jumped off the vehicle and ran away with their flashlights. When I realized that I was walking alone, I stopped to take in my surroundings. It was then that I realized that I was standing at the edge of a cliff. From afar, I saw the silhouette of a small house in the middle of a cluster of trees. In fear, I trekked back to my Jeep, hoping that somebody would come to keep me company. Hours passed and nobody came. Tired and sleepy, I sat back on the driver's seat. I had no flashlight to light my watch. I could only estimate the time to be past midnight. A few more minutes and I heard a male voice telling me, "Miss, you can go home now. The two women are staying for the night."

I immediately started the engine and felt like I was piloting an airplane. I was not prepared to drive alone in that mountainous, dark place. Suddenly, I felt my hair sticking up in the air with absolute fear. My knees started to clap in terror as I drove down the hills. That moment, I failed to trust the angels who could have come to my rescue. So many negative thoughts played in my mind. All those horrible stories that I'd heard from my childhood started to haunt my imagination.

What if I look in the rear mirror and I see a ghost in the back seat? What if the two women that I just drove to the hills were ghosts? What if the engine stops? What if my brakes go wrong? What if my headlights fail? I felt a chill snaking up and down my spine.

A few more minutes and I was surprised that I was already in the town proper. The first familiar building that I saw was my office building. Not having enough energy to drive one more mile for home, I decided to stay in my office and take a rest. I did not want to go home looking scared. Otherwise, my mom would never again let me drive alone at night. My mom was always concerned about my Jeep breaking down when I was alone in the dark. I never listened to her.

It was one o'clock in the morning. I remembered that the guard who was supposed to be on duty had not reported for work because of a family emergency. To be all by myself did not concern me that much because I knew that I was already in town and almost home.

After a glass of water and a number of deep sighs, I decided to go home and tell my mom exactly what happened that night. No need to tell a lie, I thought. I butted my chair away and walked out the door and back to my vehicle. I made three attempts to start the Jeep, but it would not turn over. On my fourth try, all the lights around me suddenly went off. Total darkness enveloped the whole town. For a few seconds, I could not see anything around me. I wanted to yell for help, but who would be there in the silence of the night? To the sides were school buildings and business establishments. Farther behind me was the ocean. If I walked to the nearest residence, who would be awake to open the door for me? Besides, I could drive but not walk in the dark.

This time I was too weak to panic. I rested my hands on the steering wheel as I surrendered my fears to God in prayer: "Lord, You are the only one who knows about my present predicament. Please send someone to help me."

Slowly, the white paint of the old Spanish church became visible in the darkness. This time, I was not scared. I started to pray fervently, while fixing my gaze on the 200-year-old church.

Suddenly, I saw somebody walking toward me. He was holding a bright lamp and a box, and his strides were swift and sure, as if he knew about my plight. He asked, "What's the problem?"

"My engine wouldn't start," I replied. He put down his toolbox and his lamp and, without saying anything more, he opened the hood of my Jeep and started to fix the engine.

From the side, I could see that his face was round. He was wearing a red cap, a white shirt, dark short pants, and a pair of slippers.

He closed the hood and gestured for the key. The engine started right away. He immediately took his lamp and his toolbox and walked briskly away. I was just preparing to reach for my purse to pay him, but in a flash he was gone. I looked around and I saw no traces of him. I said "Thank you," and somewhere in the dark, I heard a faint "Welcome."

As I drove home, I started to wonder about the auto mechanic who came to help me. So many thoughts started to dance about in my mind. *Why did I not ask for his name? Where did he come from? Who sent him to me? At past midnight, what was he doing in the streets with a toolbox and a lamp?*

I reached home around two o'clock in the morning. My parents were still awake, waiting for me. My dad told me that they had searched the whole town for me. After hearing my story, my mom confidently said that she believed in her heart that the angels were truly with me that night.

Since that mystery happened, whenever I came home late, my mom would jokingly say, "I guess you helped deliver a baby again!"

That night I went to bed hoping that the next day I would find the man who came to my rescue. I was thinking that I could give a vivid description of him to my sister, who, being an engineer, traveled everywhere and knew most, if not all, of the auto mechanics and handymen in town.

The following day, I was saddened to hear that my sister knew nobody who fit my description. In the next few months, until I left my home town, the two of us drove around the auto mechanic shops and everywhere around the island, but our search was in vain.

To this day, I get chills whenever I remember that particular hopeless and moonless night when an angel came to help me.

A Thought

At the hillside, I failed to call on God. Instead, I dwelled on scary thoughts that enslaved my whole being. When my vehicle would not start, I put aside my fears and trusted God instead. I called on Him and He immediately sent an angel to help me.

Prayer

Lord, may I never underestimate the power of prayer. May I always believe that prayer is my direct channel to you.

FOUR

Confounded by a Little Boy

JC Narag

The little brown thing squealed day and night from a backyard pig pen. It was a baby pig given to me by my friend Jolie. It was my share from the mother pig she got from me on a loan. The sow gave birth to three. So my friend had two and she gave me the third. The baby pig was about two months old.

Barney was only skin and bones and his eyes were big and protruding from their sockets like the buttons from Grandpa Ken's coat—ready to fall anytime.

One look at Barney was enough to start my day in the wrong direction. And the stink from his temporary quarters made me dizzy and sick to my stomach.

"Will someone help me get rid of Barney? His name is the only good thing about him! He adds to all the rubbish in this world. He is pollution personified," I cried out as I was preparing for work.

Alex, my four-year-old son at that time, came to me and said, "He is so tiny, he deserves some pity. He has to have a decent home now that his mother is not there to feed him and give him warmth."

"Let's deposit him in the pig pen. That's the best. The boar and the others will give him a round of disciplinary measures," I continued.

"He can't survive in the pig pen," my husband Nick chimed in, half in jest. "He won't be allowed to eat or sleep. That's the surest place to silence him fast. But you know, after two months, with proper care, he will be just right for roasting in time for your birthday."

"Let me not have anything to serve on my birthday if it has to be Barney. I am serious. Please, let's get rid of Barney. Perhaps we can just leave him at the side of the flood drainage when the rain comes. Barney's pollution can't let me think straight this time," I said and left for work.

When I came home from work later in the day, Alex met me at the gate.

"Someone is taking Barney home and so we don't have to let him die in the flood control," he said. I could tell by his red eyes that he had shed a tear for Barney. I patted his back and told him that I also pitied the pig, but I really could not bear the earthly purgatory he was giving me.

My heart melted with pity and beat like a thousand tom-toms as I watched Alex give Barney a last fond embrace before putting him in a sack.

One more time, I felt this way when Alex was a little older:

I was getting ready for my part-time teaching job when I heard a tiny voice speaking in a most tender, loving, and caressing tone. I turned off the water tap, as it was competing with another voice. Someone was telling me that Alex was talking to our six newborn kittens.

Mings, our mother cat, chose a drawer left ajar by my oldest daughter, Mercy. Here, Mings gave birth to six kittens. Mercy's shirts and her special things were soiled beyond repair, and so was the drawer beneath it, where my younger daughter, Grace, was keeping her first love letters. The birth stains were impossible to deal with. Six-year-old Grace cried when she saw the love letters stuck together, including a love letter she got from four cousins who said in one common letter that they loved her. Marinela, the third girl, pouted as she inspected the third drawer, to make sure nothing there was spoiled.

The smell from the drawer hurt our nostrils. There was also a lot of noise, as the mother cat and the six kittens meowed endlessly. Most of all, the air was heavy with the stink coming from the cat house put up for them by Alex.

I gave Alex an ultimatum. "Get rid of the kittens—fast. Take them to the farthest farm. See that they don't come back. Or put them in a sack and leave them at the seashore. They can survive on mice there. Or just leave them in the wilds," I said with finality.

"I will not come home for lunch today if the bastards will still be here!" I called out from the gate as I left for work.

In my heart I pitied the little monsters, but I was still smarting from a foul morning triggered by these newest intruders. I did not come home for lunch, but I was praying that the little ones would still be there when I got home.

Mid afternoon I came home and my heart beat double time when I found that the house was in deep silence. The familiar meows were missing. I went straight to the cat house. And that's when I heard Alex talking to the kittens in that very tender, loving way. I listened carefully.

"Don't be sad," Alex said. "I have found new homes for you. You will be taken good care of there. I will miss you, but I promise to visit each one of you as often as I can."

Lined up on Al's extended arms were the kittens, three on his left and three on his right.

"Don't forget I love you all!" Alex whispered as he put them down.

I was going to embrace Alex to tell him I was so sorry…and that we were keeping the kittens. But first, I wiped the tears that were now blurring my vision.

Alex came out breathless. "Ma, I have contacted six families in the neighborhood. Each of them will take in one kitten. You don't have to suffer because of them. I pity them and I'll miss them, but I'm sure they will have a good life."

With goose bumps running down from head to toe, I embraced my son and apologized profusely. I assured him I was not that unkind and cruel. My stomach was just too weak for the foul smell and my patience was short for all the trouble they were giving us.

Then I gave way to warm tears—shed not only for Ming's poor kittens, but most of all for my ugly ways that hurt the tender and finer feelings of my little son. I resolved never to be unkind to animals, especially to baby animals.

A Thought

Alex's love and compassion for animals touched my heart as a mother.

Prayer

Lord, as I make decisions that benefit only myself, may I be careful not to hurt a loved one's feelings.

FIVE

The Hug of Little Darius

Thalia Narag Cayetano

Catechism is a study of the basic teachings of the Catholic Church.

Thursday at noon was my dedicated time for God. In three months, I would be leaving the city to start a new job in my home town. I promised God that I would go to church every morning, and spend two hours a week before the Blessed Sacrament to thank Him for giving me the opportunity to serve the people in my town.

Standing in front of the church was Father Andre, who was talking to one of the elders.

"Good morning to you both," I said as I took Father Andre's hand to kiss.

"It's you!" Father Andre said in a loud voice. "What's your name again?" Confused, I told him my name. He said, "Thalia, God has chosen you to teach catechism in one of the classes that we are offering for kids this summer. The teachers are meeting in my office now."

Thinking of the time that I was already missing at the Blessed Sacrament, I could not move or say a word for a moment. Slowly, although my spirit was unwilling, I walked to the room where the meeting was being held. Father Andre was one of my favorite priests and saying no to him was a hard thing to do. He walked behind me to introduce me to the catechists. Filled with terror, I wanted to announce to everyone that I hadn't ever taught a religious class before. I wanted to tell them that I was there because I was too shy to say no to Father Andre. Unspoken words hung in the air. I just did not have the boldness to open my mouth to speak. A young man who introduced himself as Lino seemed to notice my apprehension. He smiled at me and whispered, "If this will be your first time teaching catechism, don't worry. We will be given a teacher's guide to follow. Besides, if you want, I can be with you to assist you on your first teaching session."

I was assigned to teach the poverty-stricken children on Hale Street. I learned from Lino that nobody wanted to volunteer to teach these kids because they were filthy, wild, and ill-mannered. He further said that in the past, volunteer catechists started the class but got discouraged and would not finish.

I was moved when I heard this. A riveting interest to teach the kids suddenly replaced my apprehension about teaching without experience.

The night before my first meeting with my students, I started to read the teacher's guide and began to practice talking in front of the mirror. I felt awkward at first, but love removed any fear or shyness.

Both excited and nervous, I brought in my small sound system and a microphone to the little chapel where the class would be held. To my surprise, I saw the little place packed with kids whose ages ranged from three to fifteen.

"Weren't my students supposed to be from ages nine to fifteen?" I turned to Lino. One of the mothers who heard my question stepped closer and said, "The younger ones that you see in this room are the little brothers and sisters of the older ones. They wanted to join because they knew that snacks will be served after each class."

That explains why they are holding cups, plates, and utensils, which they brought from home, I thought.

"Who feeds them?" I asked.

"Whoever among the parents is willing to spend for their snacks that day. We usually serve juice, noodles, or pastries. If nobody offers, then the kids do not eat."

My heart was torn into pieces. I wondered if there would be a parent who would allow that to happen. But I knew that life was hard for the families in that area. Only a few of the kids' parents were earning money at that time.

Three weeks passed, and I felt like I had lost several pounds from too much sweating. Standing and talking for three hours a day, five days a week, in front of seventy-seven kids with such an age range was a real challenge.

One day, when summer was at its peak, I suddenly felt suffocated, as if I were running out of oxygen. The small chapel was packed with people and only had a few windows. I took a deep breath and stopped talking for awhile. All of a sudden, a three-year-old boy walked toward me from the back of the chapel. His nametag identified him as Darius. He stared at me and smiled. I noticed right away that he had a runny nose. He hugged my thighs tightly for a long time, and I could hardly move. I caressed his curly hair and stooped down to reach for him. As I held him up, I noticed that his nose got cleaned out after he hugged my thighs. With an innocent look, he started to wipe my perspiring face with the napkin that he was holding. All the other kids laughed and one of them yelled out, "The napkin isn't clean! He used it already!"

"It's okay," I said. "He didn't know."

From that day on, Darius became one of my favorite kids in the class. I would call his name and he would just come up in front to give me a comforting hug. His hug became the fuel that energized my body. His expression of pure love was the air that reinforced my spirit.

When the summer catechism was almost over, a non-Christian friend of mine teased me, saying that I was missing the real summer fun by spending too much time with my students. Little did he know that being with the poor children had been the most interesting happening in my life!

Every day, after the three-hour class, some of the kids would walk with me to where I lived. Others would follow later. Their parents entrusted them to me and would not look for them until it became dark. After they left, I would get my book and study for the following day's lesson.

What was particularly amazing was that the little ones tried to behave well, including Darius. I realized that they did not join the catechism just for the food that was being served after class, but they were there to feed their souls, too! Soon, I started to simplify the teaching method and the words that I used. I made sure that a statement that was well understood by a fifteen-year-old could also be readily understood by an eight-year-old and a three-year-old. In the next weeks, some of the younger ones started to participate in the class by asking innocent questions about God. It was inspiring to see them becoming more familiar with the Catholic prayers, and a lot of the stories from the Bible. Soon after that, the children started to exhibit a total reformation. The more love and attention given to them, the better they performed. Soon, the once unruly kids on Hale Street became more gentle and refined. They became an inspiration to other kids in the slum areas. Many people heard about the children from the small church who had great faith, and they started to give moral and material support.

On Saturday mornings, the children started their day early by walking to the nearest church to attend the 5:30 a.m. Mass. After church, we would all walk to a nearby food chain for breakfast. They took turns telling stories about their families and friends. Little Darius never failed to say something about his family.

On Sundays, we would gather at three in the afternoon to rehearse songs for the six o'clock Mass. Imagine a choir of seventy-seven singers. Voices were separated by tone, timbre, and age, but the children sang from the heart in unison. People who attended the Mass did not mind standing outside the chapel, for the choir occupied most of the seats.

Because the kids were in the house almost every day, my sisters and brothers started to care for them too, making sure that their after-class snacks were being served.

Finally, the catechism class was over. It was time for me to leave the city for my home town. The children continued to communicate with me by sending letters. The little ones, including Darius, sent their drawings.

On Valentine's day, I received a card from Laura:

Dear Thalia,

Whenever we see or hear an airplane roaring high above the houses on Hale Street, some of us run out to the streets and call out your name at the same time. That is how much we miss you. I hope you will come visit us soon. I am sending you red hearts with our names and notes on them. We save money so we can buy stamps to mail you letters every week. We still go to church and sing in the choir even without an accompaniment. We have been trying to be good, including Darius. I am now in sixth grade. Gail, Rosie, Lance, and Paul are my classmates. One of our teachers asked what we did last summer to make us better kids. I told her that we learned about God and we learned how to love and experienced being loved in return.

Thank you for loving us for what we are.
Always,
Laura

The poor kids on Hale Street continued to be a part of my life. My passion to care for the less fortunate kids grew. And it all started with the hug of little Darius.

A Thought

The old ones stood in awe as the children persevered in their faith. The rich were humbled when the poor gathered in love.

Prayer

Lord, teach me to love and to judge not by human standards, but by your standards. Help my heart to know that every human being deserves to hear about the kingdom of God—the young, the old, the rich, the poor, the good, and the bad.

Six

His Father's Oscar

JC Narag

Oscar remembers very well those times he and his two younger brothers, Ron and Ed, would ravage the garbage heap near his village by the sea. Ron was four and Ed was five. The three were forever looking for some of the thicker strips pared off from vegetables and root crops by some careless cooks.

Some lucky days, half or even whole small tubers or pieces of sweet potatoes would fill their bucket—and there would be more than enough for lunch for their mother, who was nursing her thirteenth child, and ten other siblings. There were two high school students, seven attending grade school, and four homebodies—children who were not attending school.

Oscar was two years overdue for grade one, but he had to stay home to take care of Ron and Ed, who were habitual fixtures of the brook just a thin wall away from their house. Lisa, the girl next to Oscar, was tomboyish and taking care of kids was not her thing. She preferred to climb trees, scale rocks, or play "kick the can" with the neighborhood bullies.

Most days, the thicker strips pared from the root crops would be washed carefully, spoiled spots taken out, the outermost layers peeled off, dumped into a cooking vessel, boiled, and mashed for lunch.

Oscar's mother, Lally, always had a baby to nurse, ever since he could remember. And his father? His father, Pando, had a regular job at the local public works office and his salary was some steps above the regular wages at the time. But he was addicted to gambling and girls. Oscar called him "my father, the lover boy."

Lover Boy brought home practically nothing for his legitimate family. He came home only to cause the birth of a new baby. But Lally was a most patient woman and women's liberation, or women's rights, never crossed her mind.

When Oscar was in secondary school, his playboy father stopped coming home. Word got around that he was living in a tree house in the jungle. He was also seen in lots of unlikely places—in fishing villages, in farmhouses, in his girlfriends' houses, in the dance halls, or at wedding parties—but never in his own home.

He was still holding his old job. And he had this new girlfriend, a teenager younger than his oldest granddaughter.

Oscar and his older brothers never gave up on their father. One morning, they visited him in his tree house. From the ground, they asked him to give just a few pesos for the school expenses of the youngest three children.

Pando plunged from the tree house, whistling a favorite tune. Without saying a word, without even looking at his three teenaged sons, he mounted his horse and galloped through the wilderness. The three young men stood still to watch their father until the horse's neighing became too faint. Three more times, the young men tried to ask their father for some help, but he never favored them with even a silver coin.

The first Sunday after reaching the mandatory age for retirement, Pando was unusually happy but thoughtful. Days before, he had been telling a friend that he was worried about getting old. The sign of old age was creeping down his spine and was giving him cold feet. Would this mean the girls would be harder to catch? He was asking himself this question often.

He got on his horse one aimless day and shoved off. Where to, he did not know. At sunset, he was still riding around. He gave his horse a strong lash. The horse tripped and Pando fell into a ravine. Some kind souls brought him home on a sled.

Nobody was in the old house. Pando's wife had died five years earlier. All the children had left the coop. Four of them lived in rented houses nearby. But none of them came around to see their father. Only his young girlfriend came often to feel into his pockets for any cash or valuables.

Oscar lived with his family on a farm five kilometers away. He was the last to know about his prodigal father's return to the village. He learned that neighbors took turns to feed the old man and to attend to his personal needs. Oscar asked his wife to prepare a packed lunch for two. He brought along some shirts and pants and fresh sheets, and proceeded home to see his father.

Oscar was met by one brother and three sisters some distance from the old house. In unison, the four cried out, "Just leave the old man alone. He has never loved us. He let us suffer while he squandered his money. He doesn't deserve any help, much less any love."

The young man stood speechless for a moment, but his lessons in Ethics 1 came to him in a flash, and the voice of his teacher rang clear in his ears: "Remember class, God's fourth commandment—'Honor your father and your mother.' This commandment does not say, 'Honor your father and mother if they are good.' Therefore, no matter what kind of parents you have, you must honor them. Give them the respect and dignity that they deserve. Don't forget, this is God's commandment, not mine."

Oscar raced to see his father. A long and warm embrace took the place of a conversation. He bathed him and put on his fresh clothes. He changed his sheets and served him the packed lunch prepared from the farm by his wife. His first words to his father were an assurance that he would take care of him from then on. As Oscar was telling him how he had missed him and how great he felt talking to his own father, the old man opened his eyes and held him close. "I was right when I chose your name," he said. "You are my 'Oscar.'" These were the last words that escaped from his father's lips. He lived for a few more days, and then died in his sleep.

Oscar went on talking. "Excuse me, ma'am, for stealing some of your time by telling you this long story about my family. You see, I volunteered to deliver the bed you ordered. I had to tell you this story—which is my tribute to you. Your words in our ethics class never fail to touch me each time I think of fathers and sons.

"By the way, what does my name, Oscar, mean? I did not understand very well what my father meant," he continued.

"An 'Oscar' is that gold-plated statuette awarded every year by the Academy of Motion Picture Arts and Sciences of Hollywood, U.S.A., for the highest achievements in film production. It is a first-class award. You are what your name denotes—an award of the highest quality—an 'Oscar,'" I answered.

"Thank you, ma'am," Oscar said, and stood to leave. He tripped twice on the stone-lined path. As he looked back to wave goodbye, I could see clearly, tears rolling down his cheeks.

A Thought

Tell people about the upright things that you know. You may never know when your words may soften a stony heart or change a well-structured plan, a solid decision.

Prayer

Lord Jesus, help me to honor my earthly parents as you honor your Father in heaven. Set my heart to love so I can easily forgive.

SEVEN

God Teaches the Humble

(A Miracle of the Blessed Sacrament)
Thalia Narag Cayetano

Cursillo is a three-day study of Christianity. A person who finishes the class is called a Cursillista. A Cursillista may assist in any future Cursillo class that is sponsored by the church. One may choose to join the music ministry, to offer janitorial or messengerial services, or help in the kitchen to serve and prepare meals for the candidates.

The Blessed Sacrament, also known as the Holy Eucharist, is Jesus Christ's Body and Blood under the appearance of consecrated bread and wine. Catholics believe that when Jesus' words at the last supper are repeated by a priest during the holy sacrifice of the Mass, by virtue of those words, the bread and wine become the consecrated Body and Blood of Christ. The Blessed Sacrament is normally exposed for public devotion and adoration through a vessel called monstrance. Worshippers are encouraged to pray and genuflect before the Blessed Sacrament to honour the real presence of Christ.

A tabernacle is a structure in the church where the Blessed Sacrament and consecrated Host for communion and ministry to the sick are kept. The tabernacle is usually set upon a side altar of the church or the altar of a special sacramentary chapel.

It was a busy day in the Cursillo center, and it was my first time assisting in the kitchen. I hardly knew anybody in the roasting room, but I knew that all hands were moving for the love of God. We believed in our hearts that when the three-day class was over, God would be thanking each of us for having brought a number of souls to His banquet.

When the first day of the class was over, I walked quietly to my little bed. I was just about to say my evening prayers when Linda, one of the facilitators, came to me and said, "Thalia, tomorrow we need you to give a talk on one of the topics, 'The Blessed Sacrament.' We just got word that the assigned speaker for this topic can't make it for tomorrow's session."

"This is a big joke," I said with a smile. "I could never imagine myself talking to a crowd about something that I do not have a vast knowledge about."

"Yes, you do. Your experience will dictate to you what to say. If you believe in the real presence of God in the Blessed Sacrament, then you will have something to say. I will give you a handout that will basically define the meaning of the

Blessed Sacrament. Expounding on it will be your job. Make sure that your talk will not last for more than twenty minutes." Linda's serious look scared me.

I looked at the paper that she gave me and it contained two short paragraphs about the subject matter. Almost angry, I said, "If I read what's in this sheet, it would not even last a minute. What am I going to say for the rest of the twenty minutes? Why do you put so much confidence in me, when I myself don't have any self-confidence? I am here to work in the kitchen and not to talk to a crowd."

Linda looked at me with all sincerity. "God has confidence in you. Your schedule to talk is at nine o'clock in the morning. Thirty minutes before that, I suggest that you pray in front of the Blessed Sacrament. Ask God to fill you with the Holy Spirit so that He will pour into you the right words to say."

I was not able to say anything anymore. She left when my eyes started to give her signs that I was ready to retire for the night.

"My Father, I am so weary. Forgive me if I am not able to recite my evening prayers from the heart. Please let my love for you abound so that nothing can stop me from doing your will. I ask this in the name of Jesus, my savior."

The morning sun was bright and certain, fixing its rays on the Cursillo house. The candidates, after saying grace after breakfast, were singing some familiar Cursillo songs. It was thirty minutes after eight. With my mind almost empty, I walked swiftly to the Sacramentary Chapel. I took off my shoes and walked with my knees toward the Blessed Sacrament. I took a deep breath as the delicate perfume of white lilies lingered in the air. I looked straight in front of the room. On one side of the tabernacle stood a big candle as a sign of the living presence of God. Hanging in the background was a crucifix. My eyes fixed on the tabernacle, I prayed:

"Lord, I am nothing compared to you. I am going to talk about your presence in the Blessed Sacrament, but who am I to be worthy to speak about you? Yet, here I am, Lord, trusting that my love for you is enough to make me speak. Clean up my heart, my God, until the only thing that is left is my faith in you. Please give me the wisdom of Moses and the speaking prowess of Aaron."

After saying this prayer, I started to feel warmth all over my body. For a few seconds, I lowered my face to the floor to acknowledge the presence of the Holy Spirit. When I lifted my head, I was surprised to see the golden doors of the tabernacle wide open. A thick, sizzling mist coming from the tabernacle started to blur my vision. Still on my knees, I moved forward to take a closer look at the inviting phenomenon. As I approached to look closely, a warm and powerful wind hit me in the face and made me fall back to the floor. I started to cry in fear and shame. That moment, I knew that God wanted to prove to me that His presence was alive in the Blessed Sacrament; and that I need not fear for He would be with me. I got up and looked at my watch. It was exactly nine o'clock. When I went out the door, one of the leaders met me. Her hand holding mine, we started walking to the classroom. My steps were light but full of confidence.

I walked straight to the podium, introduced myself, and that is all that I can remember in detail. God took over and He used my lips and guided my thoughts to speak only the truth. As I talked, I saw some of the candidates shedding tears.

By instinct, I looked at my watch again and I was amazed to notice that my talk lasted exactly twenty minutes. I remember saying my final words, and then I walked out the door.

All in tears, the Cursillo leaders met me with an embrace. Deep in our hearts, we all understood that God teaches the humble, and that He alone can give wisdom.

A Thought

This experience has taught me that there is no room for pride and selfishness if God is truly present in the heart.

Prayer

Lord, when I ask you to rule over my heart and my mind, may I learn to empty myself of any selfish desires so you can fill me with your love and wisdom.

EIGHT

I am Always at Your Side

JC Narag

There's one very special room in my house. It used to be my three eldest daughters' room. It is just big enough to hold three beds, a table, which also serves as a dresser, and a closet. I've always kept this room immaculately clean, and only very close relatives and friends are privileged to occupy this room. On its wall beside a special window hangs a life-sized sculptured replica of the Risen Christ.

Now that my eight children, except the youngest two, are no longer in the house, this room is almost always vacant. However, when I want to be alone, this is where I go—to read or write or to just enjoy some solitary thoughts. It is here where I feel most secure even when I am alone at night. But I used to be afraid to be alone—even in this room.

One moonless night I wasn't prepared to be alone. It was the third night in a row when I slept

53

alone. My husband, Nick, was in the city on official business and all my children were there, too—working, or looking for work, or studying in college. For three nights, our young boy helper did not come home. He had just discovered the joy of being with peers, so he preferred to spend the whole night with them.

Earlier that particular night, the boy had been home at eight. I'd asked him to sleep on the front end of the structure that holds the piano, because that was near the special room.

Twice before midnight, I peeped into the area where I'd asked the helper to sleep. He was not there, but I could hear him and his friends talking and singing in the neighborhood. So I went back to sleep.

I was in deep slumber when I felt a cold, cold hand on the small of my back. I could feel the cold hand slowly moving, and finally gripping my waistline, as I lay on my side.

"Lord," I shouted. "Help me! Help me, please! I am so afraid!"

Suddenly, I was not afraid anymore. A general calm enveloped me. I turned my eyes toward the walls opposite my bed and looked up to the ceiling. These areas were all covered with a light blue mist and dotted with some star-like sparklers. I felt completely at peace. I experienced a glorious, heavenly feeling. "Alleluia!" I whispered. "Lord, I do not mind if you take me now."

As I was in this euphoric state, I felt a presence in the room. I lifted my head, and there, a little to my left, and about a meter away from the headboard of my borrowed bed, was a young man who looked like the Lord Jesus Christ of the Divine Mercy.

"Lord, I know that's you. I am so sorry I'm always afraid, especially in the dark. I even fear fear itself—as if I did not believe you are always at my side," I stammered.

"Don't ever, ever be afraid. I am always at your side," He assured me.

I roved my eyes around and I saw a big tree to the side. I could almost touch the brown, scarred trunk and the tiny heart-shaped leaves.

"What a beautiful tree! Did you also bring that in, Lord? Through the window?"

"Yes!"

After that, He vanished. I quickly asked, "Lord, Lord, are you going to take us all to heaven when we die?" I wanted to talk with Him more; I wanted Him to talk to me more, but he was not there anymore. I made an effort to get up, but I couldn't.

It was already eight o'clock in the morning when I woke up from a long, peaceful sleep. I ran to the priest's residence, then to my closest friend's house to tell her about my beautiful experience.

I get shivers every time I recall or talk about my short, short encounter with the man I believe was Jesus Christ, our Lord.

A Thought

This experience has given me a blessed assurance that God is always at my side. All I need to do is call on Him and believe in His loving presence.

Prayer

Lord, give me back the faith of my childhood. Make me as trustful as a child.

NINE

Jolted by an Earthquake

Thalia Narag Cayetano

" I am so glad you are able to be with us tonight," Aunt Mary said as she met me at the gate.

"Oh, Auntie, I'll be staying with you for a week to enjoy you and Mom while she is here in the city. I'll be commuting from here to school every day until Mom flies back home," I replied as I embraced and kissed Aunt Mary.

The highlight of my college days was when both or either of my parents came to the city for a business trip. To me, it was more special than a school break. Long before their trip, I would ask my older brother to send a permission letter to the nuns in the dormitory to allow me to be away for a certain period of time.

On July 16, 1990, the sky was proclaiming a bad day. The rain was pouring as lightning dashed and thunderclaps rolled and rumbled. The boisterous sound outside was a hint that I should be staying home. I knew that the university campus was deluged with knee-deep water every time it rained hard.

My mom, who was reading the newspaper, was unperturbed by the nasty weather. I said, "Mom, I have an exam scheduled for today but I'm deciding not to go." My mom, being a teacher herself, always reminded us that school attendance was important to a teacher.

"As long as you know that it's possible for you to be given a make-up test," she said with a trusting tone.

I was not happy with my decision to stay home. Strange enough, the sun was forcing its way through the clouds amid the rain and thunders. If the rain suddenly stopped, the majority of my classmates would show up in class and the teacher would push through with the test.

"Bye, Ma. I changed my mind. I am going to school," I said as I rushed to open the gate. I got on the first bus that stopped in front of me and started to say a short prayer.

I was a few miles away from school when, suddenly, the bus started shaking vehemently sideways. At first I thought the bus was trying to strain its way through a rocky part of the road. I looked outside the window and I saw people on the streets in a riot, screaming and running away from the buildings. The bus stopped. People in the bus screamed, "It's an earthquake!" I later saw at least fifteen nuns from the Dominican Order, holding each other's hands on the side of the road, their eyes closed in prayer.

A few more seconds and the violent shaking stopped. Finally, I was in front of my school. The earthquake had stopped, but the commotion in the campus terrified me. I felt too weak and nervous to get up. I was too scared to see the worst. The bus driver announced that he was turning around to take a trip back to our place right away. My first instinct was to stay in the bus and go home to my aunt's place right away, or stay in the dormitory for the night. But suddenly, my attention was caught by the helpless patients who were being pushed out by the stampede of people rushing out from the university hospital. Patients in wheeled beds and wheelchairs scattered all over the campus. Still in fear, I decided to see what was going on.

I stopped to take a glance at a pathetic old man whose eyes were closed, and an IV drip attached to his arm. Instantly, my heart was filled with love and compassion like never before. I started to say a prayer:

"Dear God, bless this man in front of me. Let him feel no fear. If he has never prayed to you before, teach his heart to call on you now. Please Lord, if he has to die in fear, take him into your kingdom. I ask this through Jesus Christ our Lord. Amen."

After praying for the first sick person that I saw, I prayed for the next one. I was filled with the Holy Spirit and I felt the love in my heart blossom into its fullness. I continued to walk, stop, and pray for every helpless patient that I saw. Slowly, I felt my body rise from the ground. I was walking on air! But it was no big deal to me because my focus was to pray for the helpless patients at that moment of distress.

Because I did not have to walk with my feet, in just a few minutes, I finished praying for all the people in the wheelchairs and beds that were dispersed all over the campus. Still flying, I moved toward the back of the building to look for other helpless patients who might have come out from the emergency exits of the university hospital. There were only a few people on that side of the campus. Suddenly, I felt my feet dropping down with a big thud to the ground. It was then that I started to wonder. I was actually walking in the air! *Did anybody see me? Did I scare people when they saw me flying in my school uniform? Well, I guess not. I hope not.* Shocked by the extraordinary experience, I sat on a bench under a tree and started to cry out loud, "Lord, I love you! I don't know what else to say at this moment. I am just so filled with love!" I cried and cried until somebody who thought I got hurt touched my right shoulder to comfort me. I never told her about my unusual experience. Who would believe it, anyway?

When I got home, I was happy to see everybody in the house. The phone was dead so I quietly sat beside my mom to watch the evening news. I closed my eyes and prayed for the victims and their loved ones. *Am I not lucky that I am not one of those who are mourning for a loved one tonight?* I thought.

Later that night, I decided to tell one of my sisters the soaring experience that I had. A few months after my mom had left for our home town, I wrote her a very heartfelt letter. I told her about my dreams for the family as well as for the poor and the desolate. I knew in my heart that the shaking put my little selfish world to an end. The heart that used to beat only for my immediate family and for the people within my reach began to spread its ardor to others as well. My heart was jolted to love by a 7.0-intensity earthquake.

A Thought

In the midst of that great commotion, I forgot about my own fears and stopped to pray for the helpless. Praying was the only thing that I could do for them, but it was actually all they needed. This experience made me believe that love can really work wonders. It also showed me the importance of praying for other people.

Prayer

Lord, as I worry about myself in the middle of a disaster, may I manage to calm down in tranquility and think of people who might need my love and my prayers.

TEN

Two Shirts for Kolin

JC Narag

It was the feast day of St. Anthony, patron saint of our town. As a practice, everyone had something new to wear for the day.

Being the youngest, I expected a new dress, but I just got a new pair of sandals. My left sandal was missing when we got to town so Kolin, my father's elderly farm hand, had to go half a kilometer back to try to locate it. But Kolin did not mind. He was in high spirits because he was the only one who got two new special gifts for the fiesta—a plain blue shirt from my oldest brother, Kopi, and a fine checkered polo from my oldest sister, Pancha. The two were already earning wages—Kopi was assistant manager of the agency in charge of American rehabilitation goods, and Pancha was a teacher. Both of them wanted to make Kolin happy. Being a "local" (for low caliber), as my elders called him, he was excited by anything new.

As usual, Kolin attended the first Mass at dawn, when everyone else was still asleep. I remember he made a lot of noise as he was preparing for church, but we thought he just was too excited about his two new shirts.

When the church bells rang for the second Mass, Kolin came bouncing home with a bright smile. He ascended the stairs two steps at a time. At the doorstep, he turned his head left and right, left and right, focusing his eyes on his forearms. My mother met him at the door.

"I told you to choose only one of the new shirts to wear for church. And you are wearing both! Why, you are even wearing the bigger shirt under the smaller one. The checkered sleeves are showing from under the blue sleeves right there on your forearms." Mother was angry but a little amused.

"Yeah, the one under had to be seen. I took extra care that it would be that way," answered Kolin.

"What? You are as old as my husband and you still don't know what's good for you!" my mother exclaimed in exasperation.

"I lay both shirts on the bench. I looked at the blue shirt and I liked it. I looked at the checkered shirt and I liked it, too. I really could not choose. I also thought of Kopi and Pancha. I decided to wear both. The one under has to be seen. I want both Kopi and Pancha to know that I tremendously admire their gifts to me and that I am extremely grateful to them." That was Kolin, and he had the beginnings of a win-win smile.

Kopi and Pancha shed a few tears for Kolin. All of us spontaneously gave him a standing ovation for his impromptu speech.

"Case closed. Kolin, you have won! Wear the two shirts the whole day!" That was my father, the ultimate judge.

A Thought

Kolin's intelligence might be sparse but his ability to value a kind act or a generous gift was never inadequate.

Prayer

Lord, help me to be appreciative of even the smallest gestures of love and kindness accorded me.

ELEVEN

My Mother's Wisdom Traveled with Me

Thalia Narag Cayetano

My mother is a well-known disciplinarian, with strong moral leadership. Because she is a college instructor in ethics and psychology, her words are often remembered by many. The house helpers who left the house many years back, as well as her college students who became professionals and successful leaders, often quote my mother's words of wisdom.

Mom had an ample opportunity to speak her mind, for aside from teaching at night, she also worked during the day as the provincial information officer. For that, she was given an hour-a-week slot at the local radio station to host a family-focused program. She believed that her mission on earth was to share her knowledge about religion and morality.

Every night, my mom, although busy with her social engagements, would impart to us the highlights of her conversations with people or from her lectures from school or the radio. She emphasized a portion of her story that would awaken our faith and love for God. Whenever she started talking, all of us would listen. My father, even while in the middle of watching a movie starring his favorite action star, Chuck Norris, would mute the television. We called this the "sermon hour." Listening to her was fun, but sometimes the significance or the applicability of her teachings was hard to imagine. A lot of times, I did not pay attention.

In the summer of 1987, I traveled to the city to pursue my college education. A few more minutes and I would be leaving the comforts of my home. Soon, I would be making my own decisions based on my own goals.

Before she took me to the airport, Mom asked me to join her in prayer in front of the altar in her bedroom. Teary-eyed, she started talking to God.

"Lord God, our Father, another child of mine is leaving home. As you have done with my other children who have left home, please take good care of her. May she not bring with her any resentment that she had in her youth and may she learn to love and forgive from the heart. May she keep all the good advice that she heard from me and her father and apply it in her life."

With heavy emotions, she paused for a while and continued. *"Lord, my daughter has received so much love in this home. Where she is going, teach her heart to continue to love in Christian holiness without expecting anything in return. When she feels lonely not receiving much love, may she learn to turn to you and she will be comforted. When difficulties seem insurmountable, let her be comforted by remembering that your son, Jesus, suffered more when He was on earth. When people do not seem to understand her, let her know that you do and she will have peace. Today, I relinquish her to you. Please have her recognize your holy presence in her heart so that when she does not find you there, she will long for you and search for you until she feels you back in her heart. This I ask through Jesus Christ, our Lord. Amen."*

I gave my mom a tight hug and said, "Mom, that was the gist of all the things that you've been telling me. Today, I promise to keep all your words and take them with me wherever I go."

As the airplane flew a few feet above the clouds and farther away from home, I knew in my heart that my mother's wisdom was traveling with me.

Today, it is close to two decades since I last heard the short version of my mom's evening sermons in the form of a prayer. Although I now live with my husband and daughter thousands of miles away from home, my mom's words of wisdom still serve as my guide. To be in a foreign country is not easy. Many times, I feel that the love in my heart is overflowing. After giving all my love to my husband and to my daughter, I feel that there is still love left to give. That is the time when I start missing my family and the community life back home. Sometimes I ask myself, "What am I doing here in a foreign land, when

there are a lot of people to love in my country?"
But when I remember my mom's teaching of
unselfish love, I come to realize that charity work
does not pick a place. Everywhere, there are people who have a craving for love and compassion.
Through my mom's words, I hear God's call to
charity. Sometimes people misunderstand and
deride me because I love too much. I turn to God
in prayer, for I know that He perfectly understands a heart that loves.

A Thought

After I left home, I started to lament the
days in my childhood when I deliberately
did not pay attention or listen to my mother's words of wisdom.

Prayer

Lord, I lift up to you all parents in the world,
that their counsel may be rooted in your wisdom. I
also lift up to you all the children, that they learn to
take heart their parents' good advice and make it
their code of ethics.

TWELVE

Ken Was a Godsend: Amen!

JC Narag

Ken-Ken entered my life when the dama de noche and the papaya in our front yard were in bloom. My husband Nick and I were enjoying a late-afternoon break under the mango tree when, out of nowhere, Ken stood right before us. He brought along a familiar aroma that neutralized the scent from the dama de noche and the papaya.

Ken-Ken was forever running his fingers through his sparse, gray hair, which was thicker on the sides. His hairline was receding and he looked old and haggard. But he was clever and he talked as if the world owed him a lot of things. Nick asked him how old he was and he quoted an old priest who said, "When you are sure that a person's age is thirty years or more, never ask him how old he is."

But anyway, Ken said that he was born that time of the year when the migratory flock of "kuyab," eagle-type birds, swooped down into the nearby towns.

"That was about sixty or seventy years ago?" asked Nick. Ken ignored the question.

Ken broke into a toothless grin and dipped his hands into the pocket of his denim shorts. He fished out something dark that was wrapped in a piece of banana leaf.

"Care for some? It's tapa, sun-dried carabao meat. I got it from the basket when Mary Dear was not looking. You know how dear her stuff sells; that's why her customers have given her that name—'Dear.'"

He started munching some of the tapa, his native bubble gum, and I found it extremely difficult to resist the temptation the old man was offering.

Ken stayed on for supper and slept on a wooden structure under the mango tree. He was still there for breakfast and the next day, and the next, and thus began a new life for him, and for my family.

Happiest about Ken were my three youngest children—Thalia, Ava, and Demy—aged four, two, and one.

The three little ones thought Ken was their real grandpa and they called him "Lolo." They shared with him every kid thing they had. They even gave him real bubble gum. Lolo was also happy to bring home to the kids anything he could get from the farm or from the rolling stores near the cockpit where he spent his Sunday afternoons.

Life with Ken was both gracious and exasperating. Some days he would come home with a sack full of citrus fruits. He said he planted these in the forest or hills where he lived after he came out of prison. Ava and Demy did not quite understand what stealing or what dishonesty was all about, so they kept asking for more citrus fruits from Lolo.

Early one morning he came home whistling, with a big, round pumpkin resting on his left shoulder. Slung on his right shoulder was a sack from which were sticking out bananas.

"These are not stolen. I found them in the middle of the sweet camote plantation," the old man volunteered.

"Return those fruits to the owners. Sweet potatoes do not bear pumpkins and bananas," my husband said. Without saying a word, Ken carried back the pumpkin and the bananas and walked out the gate. My older son Alex spied on him but did not tell us until much later that Ken sold the fruits for two bottles of hard liquor.

During lighter moments, Ken filled the house with laughter as he regaled us with his stories. He always prefaced or ended each story with "Whether you believe this or not, this is a true story."

His favorite story was his trip to China. He was a stowaway on a ship transporting ajimoto, for ajinomoto (MSG, or monosodium glutamate). One of the crew took him on that trip because he was a strong man and could load and unload cargo with ease. He was packed in a big container cov-

ered with some merchandise, including ajinomoto.

"I learned to eat with chopsticks even while
cramped in that drum," he boasted.

Another favorite story was the old man's
adventure with giant coconut crabs, "tatus," and
spirits. He promised to bring tatus to his friend,
the town judge. He had already spent one day and
one night in the mountains, but he had not found
any tatus. Then he remembered it was August,
one of those months when these crabs dig deep
into the ground to hibernate. They come out at
the break of summer in March.

So what did poor Ken-Ken do? He closed his
eyes and invoked the aid of his spirit-friends to
help him catch giant crabs because his friend the
judge was expecting him to come with crabs.
When he opened his eyes, a large purplish thing,
the size of three fists put together, was moving
toward him, two more crawling nearby. When
Ken's native backpack of woven bamboo strips
was almost full, he hurried to town.

The judge met him at the door with a wide,
wide grin. "Believe me," Ken said, "this is a true
story."

At dusk one day, Nick and I were preparing
for our classes at the local college where we both
taught, when we noticed the children talking in
whispers. Demy cupped his hands to my ear and
whispered that Lolo Ken-Ken had not arrived
home. He'd left early that morning in his one-
man wooden boat to fish with hook, line, and
sinker. Alex, my older son, had gone to the wharf

to try to locate their grandpa. The latter was not there. The little boat was not in its berth. Nick and I attended only our first-period classes. My children and I hurried along one of the roads leading to the port; Nick took the shortcut. We all returned home and there was Ken. He was talking in a most incoherent manner. But I could make out he was asking me to light a candle for him. That is to thank the Lord for allowing him to live a while longer in this beautiful world.

After gulping a hot cup of coffee, he continued his tale. On the boat, he had drifted into the open seas. He fought giant waves that smashed against his little craft. He rowed against treacherous currents that threatened to pull him toward Taiwan. All his fish were washed away.

About three o'clock that afternoon, giant waves and a strong, friendly current carried him along, until he anchored at Mahatao port, six kilometers away from Basco, his home port.

Early the next morning, we lit six candles, not just one, for Ken-Ken. When Nick and I came home from an early-morning church service, Tito, a friend from Mahatao, was waiting for Nick to get some help regarding family land problems. While waiting, Tito asked if Ken had any fish left for us from the day before. Not waiting for an answer, he said that he was sure there was no more fish left as many people had come to buy and to feast on Ken-Ken's huge catch of tuna.

Alex, the ever-compassionate boy, anticipating a confrontation with Ken later on, said, "Mom, can we just forgive Lolo for having lied to us? He told us that his parents passed away when he was a little boy and nobody taught him the right values."

But the worst was yet to come. Nick and I came home from our teaching jobs to find our house dark, empty, and silent. Finally, we located six-year-old Leah asleep on her bed. Then we found the other children, including two adopted ones, at their grandma's house, which was a few steps away from our side yard. Between sobs they related how afraid they were. Lolo Ken was drunk and the children were cheering for Uncle Ely in a billiard game. Ken came out, brandishing a jungle bolo, shouting that he was going to kill all of them. The three older ones each carried on their backs one of the three younger kids. Then they locked themselves up in their grandma's house. There they found out that Leah was left in the house. But none was brave enough to come out to get her.

Nick's decision was final: Ken was to look for another family to take him in. He could still take his meals in the house until he could find a new family.

My father, Pablo Caballero, came to the house two days later. He heard about Ken-Ken being sent away. So he asked for a dialog with me.

PC: I hear you are sending Ken away. Is that true?

JCN: Yes, because he almost killed all my children, including the two who are adopted.

PC: Did you invite or ask Ken to join your family?

74

JCN: No, he just came and stayed.

PC: People who just choose to stay with any family are sent by God. And God chooses just one family—among so many families in the world.

JCN: I hadn't thought about that.

PC: People who just choose to stay should never be sent away.

JCN: But he wanted to murder my children.

PC: You said he was drunk. Don't let him drink.

JCN: How? I will never forgive myself if he kills my children. My husband thinks the same way.

PC: God sent Ken to you. If you send him away, you have to render an accounting to God.

JCN: My God, help me with this problem.

PC: Find a solution to this problem.

JCN: I can't find any. Ken must go.

PC: Keep him in the house so he won't drink gin. If you don't allow him to go out, and he can't drink, he could just leave and you have no responsibility for that. Don't wait for God's anger to fall upon you and your family. Remember, God sent me three hopeless people to take care of. I never sent any of them away. Tell Nick about our dialog.

So Nick and I decided to keep Ken-Ken. For months, he tried to be good. He knew that he could stay as long as he would not drink liquor.

One day, he came from a town fiesta. He was obviously drunk. Without saying a word, he bundled his clothes and left. He knew that he broke the important family rule. A few days more and we got news that Ken was in a hospital with a broken arm. My grade-school kids, Thalia, Ava, and Demy, saved their allowances to buy goodies for their Lolo. Three times, they asked me to bring him home when he was discharged.

"Yes, but you know I have lots of meetings to attend. I have no time to see him and bring him home. Just bring him home with you."

The following day, the three came home with their Lolo, each holding a bag containing his clothes.

Ken tried his best again to follow the house rule—not to drink liquor as long as he was with us. When he was with his friends and could not resist the temptation of alcohol, he did not have the courage to come home. When three days passed and my three youngest children did not see him, they and one of the older ones would look for him and bring him home.

The last time he went away, Alex, my oldest son, was the one who brought him home. Ken was old and weary and he came home to stay. He sincerely promised to stop his vicious drinking.

For the next months, Ken struggled to fight his vice. His effort was one of the reasons he stayed with us almost to the day he died. He was never sent away. After all, he was a Godsend. Amen.

A Thought

Ken was a stranger whose value system was totally in contrast to my family's. The big gap that we had was bridged by the unconditional love that my children had for him and the pure love that he had for my children in return. Later on, I learned not to insist on seeing his successes but to acknowledge his efforts.

Prayer

Lord, may I always see you in the eyes of a stranger or of all the people you put in my care.

Thirteen

The Midnight Troubadour

Thalia Narag Cayetano

In my home town, there are no music schools where one can learn to play an instrument. Yet playing a tune can be easily learned by someone who has the passion for music.

Victor was a lonely, scrawny old farmer who always carried with him two precious possessions: a flashlight to light his path after midnight and a harmonica to enliven people with his music.

After a week's toil on the farm, Victor rewarded himself by drinking liquor with his peers. He went around the town to look for buddies who would be willing to enjoy the weekend with him. When alcohol started to set in, the usually shy and quiet Victor became witty, talkative, and full of energy. He recited all the English words that he knew, boasting that he was familiar with the language, though he never went to school. Particularly impressive was when he played the harmonica. Lively or mellow, his music never failed to fascinate a tuneful heart. Again, he boasted that he did not go to school to be able to play the harmonica. He said that music played by ear was music played from the heart.

Victor stopped drinking when he knew he was too drunk to go on with his literary and musical bravados. This usually happened around midnight or when his legs were too weak to give him the support to go home. Yet, armed with a big flashlight and his favorite musical instrument, he managed to crisscross the unlit streets with confidence.

But Victor's weekend zest did not end there. On his way home, he would stop by the house to ask if any of us in the family wanted to hear him play the harmonica. My brothers called him the Midnight Troubadour, for he almost never failed to come to the house at midnight to play music.

Whenever the doorbell rang at midnight, my oldest brother would get up from bed and open the gate for him. The two of them played music together. Victor played the harmonica or sometimes sang songs that he himself composed, while my brother accompanied him on the guitar. The rest of us would wake to the enthralling sound of the music. Before long, all of us would gather in the living room to enjoy the music for the next two hours.

When I left my home town to join my husband in America, Victor's music continued to linger in my mind. On my first visit to our home town, I brought him a new harmonica. The thought of having a new harmonica put his spirits to the crest, so that now he always volunteers to play a tune on special occasions like weddings or birthdays or community festivals.

Years passed and my family in our home town would tell me stories about Victor and his harmonica, which was beginning to get rusty and out of tune. When I went home for the second time, I intended to surprise him with another new harmonica. Yet during my twelve-day stay in our home town, he was nowhere to be found. A neighbor of his said that he was plowing up in the fields and maybe too tired to come home for the weekend. My vacation was over and it was time for me to fly back to the city and eventually back to America. The Midnight Troubadour never came to serenade us. I labeled the box of the harmonica with his name and gave it to my brother to keep.

I was in the city for three days, waiting for my flight back to America, but none of my family called me about Victor.

On my way to the airport that gloomy afternoon, I got a call from my brother, telling me that somebody wanted to play long-distance music for me. Amid the loud honks of buses on the highway, Victor's familiar music did not fail to stir my soul. My thoughts immediately went back to my humble home town, where life is simple and thoughts unstained, where spirituality can be easily obtained through a tune played from the heart.

Victor played three of my favorite folk songs. I was not concerned about the phone bill that my loving brother had to pay. I knew that all he cared for was to elate my spirit with Victor's music before I left.

After playing one of my requested songs, I heard Victor's pale and shy voice. I sensed right away that he was not drunk. "I can never thank you enough for buying me a new harmonica. You know that a poor man like me cannot afford to buy such a treasure. Can I keep playing music for you on the phone until distance stops me?" Twice or thrice, the music stopped because Victor was sobbing. At last, the music slowly faded until I could not hear anything.

While on the airplane with my daughter and my husband, I kept thinking of Victor and his heartfelt music on the harmonica. I was amused that a thirty-five dollar harmonica could bring a lifetime of happiness to a simple man like Victor. What a feeling to make a person happy in a very simple way! But I hope that Victor realized that hearing his music was worth more to me than the price of a harmonica.

When I got home to California, I called my brother to ask him to check on Victor's harmonica once in a while to see if it still sounds good. I made a promise to myself that I would make sure that his happiness lasts a lifetime by buying him a new harmonica whenever necessary.

A Thought

A tangible thing becomes valuable when the use of it brings an intangible worth. True love and charity can grow by giving value to

life's simplest things and to the earth's lowli-
est people.

Prayer

*O Lord, make me learn to value and respect
the little things that are important to humble and
lowly people and make me realize that they are
important to you, too.*

FOURTEEN

I Burned the Debt Notes—Dad

JC Narag

When dad was eighty years old, he told me he would give me a notebook. It had forty-eight leaves and was bound in the middle with a fine but sturdy cotton cord.

"Don't ever lose the notebook," he said. "It contains the names and the addresses of the people who borrowed money from me. The borrowers are from the high and mighty and also from the poorest of the poor."

Dad further said that about ten pages of the notebook were filled with the names of those who borrowed material things from him—farm tools like plow parts, shovels, hoes; carpentry tools like meter sticks, saws, hammers; cooking utensils such as pots and pans; articles of clothing; and miscellaneous items like horse saddles and musical instruments.

"When I die, collect payments only from those who have steady incomes, or those who are in a position to pay," he said. "Ask payback first from the borrowers whose children have finished college and are now working; also from those whose houses are now earning some money from rentals.

"As for the materials borrowed, I think you should just forget about them, except if you want some items to keep as souvenirs."

For the next two years, Dad did not remember to give me the notebook of debts.

One day, he came home with a violin and a guitar, carried for him by a friend.

"Is that the violin and the guitar some friends borrowed?" I asked.

"No, these are antiques, so I keep them well. I am bringing them to Manila with me because I know that I am not coming back to Batanes. I have a premonition that I will die in Manila."

One month after, Dad and his friend came back from Manila and with them were the antique violin and the equally ancient guitar.

Dad had three more trips to Manila with his two precious musical instruments, and a friend to help him with them. Along with the two instruments was the precious notebook of debts.

Believing that he was going to die in Manila, there was always a sentimental scene every time he bade goodbye for his trip. Dad's brood of young men friends would accompany him to Basco, eighteen kilometers away from our home town. Each of them would deliver short exposés of some recent follies encountered as they serenaded girlfriends and Dad's once-young beauties.

Some of the ladies would even shed tears as they begged Dad to come home soon.

Who was going to sing love songs for the girls and the silver-haired lovelies? Or accompany them on the guitar as they sweated it out in their monotones?

"Really," Dad whispered in my ear, "If you see the names of any of these friends in that note-book, just disregard such. They have paid their loans in terms of the happy times they have given me."

Three more years passed. Dad kept saying that the notebook of debts was locked in a special safe.

After his eighty-third birthday, Dad was confined in the local hospital. He called me one day and gave me instructions to tell my only brother and my three sisters to come together and draw lots for all his farm lots, including the two big parcels for untethered cattle. "Divide everything that I own equally among you, so I'll die in peace," Dad said. "But my money in the bank will be for Lin, your poor old sister.

"Most important of all, tell each one that none of you shall collect anything, or even say any unkind word to any of my debtors. I am convinced that these people would have paid me back if they were in a position to do so. They cannot afford to pay, period. I hope God will have in His heart some mercy on me for doing this. One last reminder—and this one is very, very important! Don't look for the notebook of debts I asked you to keep. I burned it several months ago."

Dad died in peace two days after these words. With due respect to him, his notebook of debt was buried in oblivion.

A Thought

Our goals and concerns change as we draw closer to eternity.

Prayer

Lord, teach me to desire the eternal riches of heaven more than the riches of the earth.

FIFTEEN

A Smile was All I Needed

Thalia Narag Cayetano

Year 2004 just crawled in. My body was still trying to reclaim the energy it lost from the eventful end of 2003. I started to wonder about a friend who was in a convalescent home, struggling with his failing health. I could almost see his eyes wanting to ask me when our next visit would be.

One quiet afternoon, something was prodding me to give Matt another visit.

At five o'clock, the rain started to pour. The cars were not moving, as if they were parked in the middle of the freeway. I was tempted to tell my husband to drive straight home, but I guess I was too tired to even say a word.

When we reached the convalescent home, the rain splattered more heavily. I was dismayed by the thought of getting wet when running from the parking lot to the building. I wanted to tell my husband to swerve the car home but again, I could not say a word. The two of us were both weary after the long trip. Somehow, we both had a silent understanding that at that moment we should not talk to each other, or else huffy words that we would later regret having said would come out of our mouths. Driven by our minds and not by our hearts, we both ran as fast as we could toward the building.

We went straight to Matt's room but he was not there. A nurse in the reception area told us that Matt was on dialysis and that he would be back after three hours.

I looked over my right shoulder and saw a woman in a wheelchair. She was alone and looked desolate. Her head was tilted to her side, almost touching the arm of her wheelchair. Her mouth was slightly open; her eyes were not moving but they seemed directed toward me. I smiled at her, and to my surprise she smiled back. I walked toward her, and still in her folded-over position, she said, "Thank you for that sweet smile, lady. That was all I needed."

Winter shivers traveled down my body with her unexpected reaction. I offered her some of the fruit that I had brought for Matt. I heard her speak again: "No, thank you. You are so kind, lady."

Amazed to hear her talk in such a sane or normal manner, I decided to start a conversation with her, but before I could pull a chair close to her, a nurse came to push her wheelchair quickly away.

"I hope you feel better," were the only words that I could say.

"Your smile has made me well," she said palely.

I sat again on the chair at the reception area, regretting that I did not get a chance to at least ask her name.

I wonder what she was suffering from? She looked physically ill but she seemed spiritually healthy.

I immediately realized that it was God's plan that I had gone to the convalescent home that day, despite the foul weather that almost made me stay home. God wanted me to be there that day not to see Matt but to give a smile to an old lady who said she needed it.

On our way home, the rain was still pouring but it did not matter anymore. My grouchy mood had vanished completely. My husband and I started to enjoy our drizzly trip.

While driving, my husband jokingly said, "Honey, if a smile can make an ill person well, we can come to that place again and again, even in bad weather, just to give away a smile!"

A Thought

When I saw the old lady in the wheelchair, my first perception was that she was too ill to notice a smile, but I threw her one anyway. Little did I know that along with physical medications, a smile could also make her well .

Prayer

Lord, when I think of my own sufferings, let me remember those who suffer more. May I never be too selfish to share whatever I have, be it money, talent, time, compliment, or even a single smile. Amen.

Sixteen

How Dad Married Mom

JC Narag

"What? Earrings for my wife, Iana? Good! But wait. I'll get my hammer," said Pablo, my dad.

He was in his early twenties that time, and had just married my mother, Iana. The two young lovers had wanted to get married three years back. But very strong opposition was interposed by my Grandma Kika.

"How can you marry Iana? It's out of the question!" Grandma would almost shout. "She comes from the lowest rung of society. Can't you find someone else? I don't understand why you and three of your older brothers prefer wives from this group of people—mahbu su suri!" (She meant low-class types.)

"There's no one else I want for a wife," my father always responded.

"But there are also other reasons why I don't allow you to marry Iana. You are the youngest, and by custom you will inherit the house and serve your father and me until we die. Since Iana is an only child, I know she will not be allowed by her mother to live anywhere else. Or have you decided to leave us and live in Iana's house after you marry her?"

"I don't care to have your house. I will buy a house for Iana. If Iana's mother and the couple living with them so desire, I will take them along to live with us."

"In that case, you will have no share of the farms, none of the gold, nothing from us."

"Okay, I will save from my meager salary, buy and sell cows, and raise goats to give my new family a comfortable life. I will also take care of you, but I will not live with you. I have consulted some wise men and they say that matters related to marriage, especially the choice of a mate, justify disobedience on the part of sons and daughters." With that, Dad ran off and did not come home for three days.

After a few weeks, Grandma learned that her son was seriously ill and could not even talk or get up. Iana and her mother, plus the elderly couple who lived with them, were ministering to his needs.

Grandma Kika was frantic. She and a friend walked three kilometers to Iana's village to see her sick son.

"Pablo! Pablo! Please do not die. I take back all the harsh words I said. You can marry Iana," Grandma called out from the door.

In sign language, the sick man requested a priest. As soon as the priest arrived, he prepared to anoint my sick father.

"Let me hold Iana's hand," Dad whispered to the priest. "I want to marry her before I die." So Dad and Mom were married. Mom held Dad's hand as he lay dying. The priest next administered the last sacraments to the bridegroom.

Relatives and friends came around to wait for Dad's last breath. Night came and his heart was still beating. Night and day, loved ones continued to watch and wait.

On the third day, Dad opened his eyes and asked for water. His throat was dry. His roving eyes were searching for someone.

Grandma Kika stepped back a little and said almost in a whisper, "She is here! Iana, your wife, is here! Get well now, my son."

As soon as Dad could sit up, Aunt Marie brought two pairs of Ivatan earrings for Iana as part of tradition. Walking with unsteady steps, Dad tried to reach for the hammer of Pabian, a young man living with my mom's family.

"What is the hammer for?" asked Marie.

"To pound the earrings and turn them into very tiny bits. I'll get earrings for my wife! She will never wear earrings from Mother," he told his listeners.

Two more times, Marie came back with the earrings, one additional pair each time. Each time, Dad came out with his hammer.

The story was related to me by an aunt. When I already had six children, I asked Dad why he never told me the dramatic events that attended his marriage. After confirming the story, he said he was not sure how I would take the story of how he and Mom married.

"By the way," he hastened to add, "I gave your mother more than thirty pairs of earrings in her lifetime. And don't forget. I married her and loved her with a love more than life."

A Thought

When love prevails, the heart is in control.

Prayer

Lord, teach me to stand by my words and fight for my principles.

SEVENTEEN

A Stranger's Prayer

Thalia Narag Cayetano

Spending an hour and a half before the Blessed Sacrament every Wednesday is something that my husband and I look forward to.

"Do you know that old woman?" My husband was pointing to a woman in her eighties who was wearing a white veil. "I have been seeing her for the past three Wednesdays but I always forget to mention to you what I noticed about her. Once in a while during the Mass, she looks back at us to throw us a smile," he continued.

"I noticed her today," I said. "Maybe she is just one of those happy people. You know what I mean? When the Holy Spirit moves strongly in your heart, you feel so much joy that you can easily give away anything, much more a smile. Or she could be just one of those grandmothers who remember their younger years whenever she sees a pregnant woman like me."

While we were talking about her, the woman in her eighties came over with a most beautiful smile.

"Hello, my name is Carrie," she said. "We don't know each other but I have been praying for you ever since I first saw you at the Sacramental Chapel. God has given me that mission. When I go to a place, I look for people whom I believe need prayers most, then include them in my daily petitions. I have chosen you because you are pregnant." She turned to me. "You are carrying a little soul that God has entrusted to you. He chose you to carry one of His children and so you have to be strong and courageous to endure whatever hardships you will be encountering."

I looked into the old woman's eyes and I was carried away by her sincerity. I wanted to open my mouth to speak but I was not prepared to talk. In my mind, I was wondering how she learned about the hardships that I had been going through ever since I conceived the baby in my womb. Many times during my first four months, I passed out due to dehydration. No kind of food or drink appealed to me, not even water. My body literally rejected anything that I took in. The difficult pregnancy made me quit my job.

"Carrie, I would like to thank you for choosing me as your prayer subject," I finally said. "I need prayers very badly. So many times, I feel like death has visited me. Please pray for this child. I want it to thrive although I am weak. I have no idea where it gets energy from, for it's hard for me to retain anything that I eat or drink."

Seeing that her kind intent was being welcomed, Carrie continued, "The baby's energy comes from God. In times like this, you need to have a strong relationship with Him. Keep praying that you will be able to carry the responsibilities of a Christian mother. I am eighty-seven years old and I am almost done with my life. I have been through a lot of hurts, sorrows, and sufferings as a mother but God helped me through them all. You are young and you have a challenging life ahead of you. Be steadfast in your faith and call on God always. He never fails to listen."

Amazed at the beauty and the wisdom of this old woman, all my words only came out as a body language. I smiled and nodded in agreement to everything that she said.

Before Carrie said goodbye, she gave me a tight hug and asked for my name.

"Sorry, I did not give you a chance to introduce yourselves to me. I feel like I have known you for years. God knows who I am referring to when I pray for you."

"Well, God has brought us together by your prayers," was all I said.

One more time, Carrie gave me a big hug while repeating my name.

Carrie became my praying buddy from that day on. Building faith through prayer and scripture reading was all we ever talked about.

A few more months and I gave birth to a perfectly healthy girl. Carrie was one of my special guests for my daughter's baptism. At the reception, I looked for a special seat for her, just as she gave me a special place in her heart.

To Carrie, my friend in Jesus: May God's radiant love shine upon you all the days of your life.

A Thought

How many strangers have you willingly prayed for? And how many people are willing to spend some time to pray for you?

Prayer

Lord, help me realize that one of the best gifts that I can give my fellow men is prayer. May I keep on praying until praying becomes my joy.

EIGHTEEN

Boys? Or Girls?

JC Narag

My father felt so guilty when his first-born—a girl—died shortly before her first birthday. "Was God punishing me?" He often asked himself. He had been praying for a boy and when the local midwife announced it was a girl, Dad felt bad. He felt that way for quite some time. But when the baby started to coo, Dad's heart was captured. But the bond between father and baby daughter was aborted due to the baby's sudden death.

Mom soon became pregnant again and Dad once again prayed for a boy. He believed that boys were more fun and easier to rear, and could help sooner to tend the goats and cows. What bothered him most about girls was that young teenagers were relentlessly giving birth to illegitimate children.

The young mothers and the little ones were a pathetic lot—almost always without the basic necessities of life. The kids would roam the streets with bare feet and bare bottoms. Most of the time, no one minded them.

During lean months when the weather was particularly harsh, the young mothers would work doubly hard on the farms; their sons and daughters left at home by themselves. Babies too young to move around would be lulled to sleep until late in the afternoon in the native hammocks made of sackcloth or some common sheets or blankets. Every time these babies would cry, their hammocks would be swung by their caretakers until the babies were dizzy and fell asleep again.

Dad remembered those times when the weather was unusually cruel. There were freak typhoons and non-stop rains that damaged the "ovi," those long starchy tubers. When this happened, food became so scarce that the children would race around with one another just to have a bite from the "ovi" in the hands of the few more fortunate kids.

Dad had clear pictures of this scene in his mind. This is the reason he resolved that he would have no daughter who could fall into such a pathetic situation. So he prayed harder for boys. And God heard his prayers, and blessed Dad and Mom with four boys in a row.

The four boys gave Mom a pretty tight schedule, which included frequent referee work as the boys fought for supremacy not only at home but also in the streets. Mom needed help taking care of these boys, and Pabian, an orphan, came along. He was six years older than my oldest brother,

Kopi. The two were perpetually locked in combat. Pabian gave in to Kopi's demands and whims a lot of times, but there were times he knocked Kopi down. Kopi felt bad, really bad during those knockouts. Kopi could not do anything against Pabian, so to make up for this, he knocked down all those helpless boys he met in the streets and along the school corridors. He became a bully. Dad, who was out working at the public works agency or busy with some sideline jobs like selling eggs or chickens or buying and selling goats or cows, did not have much time for the boys. When he was home from work, he would listen to the litany of errors and the petty follies and delinquencies committed by Kopi. Dad was a severe disciplinarian but Mom was a very even-tempered, patient woman. She was convinced that one disciplinarian in the house was enough. She'd never heard of such things as inconsistent discipline or role modeling. So she always waited for Dad to mete out the punishments.

At this time, Dad's reserve of patience was running out. He was now convinced that boys were difficult to raise. He thought hard and came to the conclusion that the only danger about girls is the possibility of them becoming illegitimate mothers. Well, he told himself, he and Mom would do their best to give them the proper upbringing and God would do the rest for them.

So for Mom's succeeding pregnancies, Dad prayed really hard for girls. God listened and gave the couple five girls. He had an obsession for young girls growing up properly, and marrying first before becoming mothers. "Girls," he frequently reminded us, "are like mirrors. Once their purity is shattered, it can never be repaired. Give me the favor and the honor of never seeing you suffer the miserable fate of illegitimate mothers and their children. Assure me that girls are easier to rear than boys."

"So be it," we assured him.

And with God's help, all of us five girls kept our promises. I also made this covenant live on when God blessed me with six daughters after I got married.

A Thought

If given proper education on morality, girls can strive to be pure and holy. They will not be regarded as mere sex objects when their virtuous ways become evident.

Prayer

Lord, please give parents a sense of responsibility to educate their children about everything that is righteous or virtuous. Make them realize that young women, with proper training, can be good instruments of your peace and love.

NINETEEN

How Can I Sing When I Sin?

Thalia Narag Cayetano

I don't have a good singing voice but singing songs of worship is one of my favorite things in the world to do. That is why I have been a member of the church choir at St. John's Church for the past seven years.

For someone like me who is not born with a good singing voice, it is easy to come up with an excuse when a good voice does not come out at a time when you need it most. However, this story is not a mere excuse. It focuses on a theory that is based on my own personal experience. My theory is: It is hard to sing for God when the soul is defiled with sin. Several times, I proved this formulation to be right.

When the airwaves of my soul are not connected with God's, my soul's home station, my vocal cords, are broken, too. I can tell when I am not within God's spiritual radius because my chest and throat feel tight. Too much guilt, somehow, affects the flow of blood coming from the heart to other parts of the body, thus ruining my vocal cords. This is a sign that I am not in a state of grace and that I need to be attuned to God before I can come up with a tune.

The last time I had such an experience was a few Sundays before Holy Week. It was my turn to sing the responsorial psalm. In our church, the cantor stands at the podium at the center of the altar.

In just a few minutes, the service would start. For some strange reason, I felt my heart blocked and numbed. I quickly ran to get some air and sing one line of the psalm. There was a tiny voice coming out from my throat, but it was empty and meaningless. Suddenly, I felt my throat tighten and the usually average kind of singing voice was gone.

I prayed, "Lord, I have been singing the psalm many times. Why is it so difficult for me to sing this time?"

Then I heard God talk through my conscience: "Sin is what is keeping you from singing. Your guilt is making you nervous because you feel unworthy to stand at the altar to sing for God. You have a few minutes to examine your conscience and clear out the smudges of sin. Do this and you will get your voice back."

I immediately ran to the altar. I knelt and bowed my head in shame and repentance. Like a movie unfolding before my eyes, I envisioned the sins that I had committed during the past month. "Lord," I blurted sorrowfully, "I have been lusting in my thoughts these past few days. Please forgive me. I also passed by a beggar a few days back and I did not even bother to stop to give him a compassionate look or thought, if not drop him a coin or two. I have been so self-centered lately that I have been failing to share my time with friends who need me. My mind has been so preoccupied with self-rewarding activities that I lose sight of things that are important to you. Please forgive me, Lord. I am not worthy to sing for you."

Suddenly, I felt my heart open up. As my heart opened up, my throat also loosened up. With confidence, I walked to my usual seat in the church and thanked God for giving me an important lesson when I needed it most.

After I had repented for my sins and asked God's forgiveness, I got my voice back! Hallelujah, God is good!

A Thought

I was so amazed to learn that even the voice can be lost when we lose our link to God.

Prayer

Lord, help me realize my sins all the time. May my service in church be accompanied by a clean heart and mind. Help me believe in my heart that if I lose you, I lose everything.

TWENTY

His Lips Unsealed

JC Narag

A few days before Demy's fifth birthday, he asked for a special favor—to be taken to Saint Dominic College, where he was going to spend his prep days in school.

"Let me tour the campus," he said. "Please take me to where the hooded ladies live or work. I want to see classrooms where I'll spend the next two years of my life; also the rooms where you and Papa teach in the evenings.

"I also want to see that place where Papa gets all those exciting stories he tells us at bedtime. Most of all, please take me to the section where chocolates and other fancy foods are displayed."

At the entrance to the registrar's office, the little boy stooped to literally smell the roses. He went around to admire the greenery, including the hanging hearts, the bird's nests, and all the assorted ferns and ornamentals. He did not say many words, but a litany of "Wow!" escaped his lips every so often.

Demy promptly got a name from the SDC office workers: "Boy Blue Smartie." He was in blue overalls and checkered shirt at that time.

"It's so beautiful here!" Boy Blue Smartie whispered. "With all these flowers and ornamentals! And the girls, too! Two of them are just cute. And that one in the blue micro-mini skirt has 'wow' legs."

The classrooms were inviting, with shiny hardwood floors where one could just lie down even without any mat during summer, he commented.

The preschool classrooms were special because from the door, the tip of the confident Mt. Iraya could be seen—just like the view from the porch at home. "That," the little boy said, "would make me feel I'm home."

Two more rooms were inspected and then I suggested it was time to go to the cafeteria. Demy gave me a sheepish smile. I knew he had been waiting for that invitation.

"The Coke here tastes much better than the Coke at home. Maybe this is pure—no water added," he said without batting an eyelash, and before I could offer any explanation. I really did not know that the little boy knew that I was diluting his Coke, not for the little savings it could bring but for the sake of keeping him healthier. I was a bit embarrassed, but I did not make an issue of the whole thing.

I braced myself for more questions, more comments.

Gulping down the last bit of cupcake with his coke, Demy shot the next question.

"When are you going to bake cakes and cookies? My older sisters, especially Mercy, often tell me that you used to do just that—bake cakes with flowers for decoration, and even with teddy bears."

Life was more difficult at that time. Producing cakes cost much. Those were the martial law years, and I wanted to tell Blue Boy Smartie that his father's recent salary increase as a registrar of deeds had been miserly—none had been implemented despite the four increases approved by Congress. But how could I explain such things to a little boy?

I also wanted to tell him that being the youngest, he should be enjoying lots of perks, including some baked foodstuff even if only for his birthday, but I had my hands full even on weekends. Truth to tell, as the communication officer for the province, I had countless meetings—both planned and emergency—with the village folks. There were also engagements for free shows and other group activities for farmers and fishermen. But again, how could I talk about all these to a five-year-old in a manner that would be comforting?

Time sped away fast without me realizing that my youngest son was going to school. My busy schedule robbed some of my time to enjoy my little boy at home.

"Are you just about to cry, Ma? Your eyes are red," he said as I quickly wiped my eyes with a tissue.

"No," I lied. "A wisp of hair just hurt my eyes."

Boy Blue Smartie said nothing for a while, but he seemed to be in a deep thought.

As we walked home hand in hand, a dialog ensued:

Dem: When I finish preschool, I will be in first grade, and then, I'll graduate from sixth grade. How long will that be?

Mom: You will finish grade school in six years.

Dem: What do you call the next grades after that? High school?

Mom: Yes. You will be in secondary school for four years, and then?

Dem: I'll be in college!

Mom: What will you take? What do you want to be?

Dem: I would like to be a pilot. But I'm thinking of something else, because I could hurt or even kill people and myself, too. Anyway, what grade comes after college?

Mom: There are also courses after one graduates from college, but most people wrap up their school life after finishing a college course.

Dem: I know what comes after college. It's getting a job, and getting married.

Mom: That's right! And after that?

Dem: The children come—all eight of them!

Mom: Never mind the number of children. Leave that to God! What's next?

Dem: Old age.

I thought that was the end of the life cycle the five-year-old was thinking of. But then he continued.

"Then people die and go to hell or heaven."

"Or purgatory," I wanted to interrupt, but Demy continued: "I want to go to heaven when I die. That's what I want most—in my whole life."

Reaching home was not the end of the dialog. Marinela, my third daughter, called out in jest from her room, "Hey, you and Pa are getting married tomorrow."

Demy stopped in his tracks and faced me squarely. "So you and Pa are not married! Why is it that you have eight children already?" His face alternately turned a bit purplish then whitish.

"Of course, Marinela was just teasing me. She meant that tomorrow is our wedding anniversary. Your Pa and I got married when we were in our mid twenties. Look at our wedding pictures right there," I said pointing to an album.

Demy seemed to be satisfied all was well about his parents having been married for more than twenty years already.

Just then, my cousin and friend Tasha came by for a cup of coffee. As she was enjoying her snacks, Boy Blue Smartie entertained her with endless kid-stuff tales and was also fielding a lot of questions.

Suddenly, Tasha called out from the dining area. "Come quickly; I can't answer Demy's questions this time!"

Coffee cup in hand, Tasha told me that she was able to answer questions such as "Why is it that you and Ma have the same number of children, eight in all? And why is it that each time Ma was pregnant, you were also pregnant? Now that she no longer has babies you also have stopped having babies. Why?"

"This time, Dem's question is a hard one," Tasha said. "He is asking me who made God."

I was hard pressed and I managed to just smile, as I was thinking of an answer.

"That's one of the mysteries of God, something that can't be really explained or understood well. But we just accept things like this—without any questions."

Before I could say more, Dem stood up between Tasha and me and said with finality, "You tell me that God made everything; that there is nothing he cannot do. Now I know the answer to my question. God made himself!"

A Thought

Even little children have an intrinsic sense of moral values. They also have a natural yearning to know God, the Creator of the universe.

Prayer

Lord, may I never underestimate the wisdom of a child. And like a child yearning for an answer, may I never stop searching for you until I find you.

TWENTY-ONE

What Matters Most

Thalia Narag Cayetano

I have always been enthralled by dreams. As a child, I used to stay in bed after waking up to give deep thought to whatever dream I'd had in my sleep. Experience tells me that dreams do not happen by accident. They come as messages, lessons, or warnings from God to help me focus or refocus my life to Him. The following are the dream symbols with their connotations that have guided me through the years:

Snake: guilt. I dream of snakes when I have sins that have not been confessed.

A garden of flowers: love. I dream of a garden of flowers when I feel loved or when I love too much.

Flying: faith. I dream of myself flying when my faith in God abounds or when my spiritual life is at its peak.

Flood or sea waves: sorrow, agony. When a loved one is in deep sin or is facing a difficulty.

Whispers: moral messages. To clarify a thought or doubt that I had in my mind before I went to sleep.

After praying the rosary with my family, I find it enriching to talk to God just before I close my eyes—when my mind is free from distractions. This is the highlight of my day: to talk to God as my father and friend. I believe that I live for a purpose designed by God and so I am always eager to recount to Him all the challenges and worries that I had during the entire day.

Springtime was halfway through. I took a deep breath as I enjoyed the cool and fresh air coming through the window. *It's been a long time since I last talked to my Father in heaven,* I thought.

Reporting to someone before going to sleep at night is not new to me, for this used to be a family practice when I still lived with my parents. After dinner, my siblings and I used to gather around my parents to report to them happenings that transpired in school.

For quite some time since winter, I had been too lazy to start a conversation with my Father in heaven. It was not until the night of May 13, 2004, when the cool and refreshing air of spring enlivened my spirit once again.

"My Father in Heaven, today was another great day for me. I was able to accomplish tasks that would normally have been difficult to do; I was also able to talk to my loved ones in a far-away country; and as usual, I was able to enjoy some quality time with my daughter. You certainly must have been present in my life because everything has been going on smoothly for me. But you know one thing that I noticed? Though life has been comfortable, I have not been feeling perfectly happy. Somewhere deep within my soul, I feel sad and anxious. It is only

now I know that it is you I have been missing. I have not been having real conversations with you.

"My dear Lord, tonight I want to ask you to possess my soul completely. My lifestyle is very ordinary but I want to do extraordinary things for you as a way of thanking you for loving me unconditionally. This means that I want to sacrifice a little bit more for the love of you. So many people are faced with physical and emotional distress. Compared to theirs, my sufferings are nothing. Did you do this for a purpose? Did you give me blessings so I can use them for your glory? Please do not punish me for taking your gifts for granted. I have to admit that when things go wrong, it is easier to get close to you, but when they go the way I want them to, I tend to forget you. Lord, please talk to me. I need you to direct me to do the things that you want me to do. I am not sure if I am living up to your expectations, my Lord. I am your servant. I will listen to your commands."

The sound of silence doped me to sleep, but I wearily continued, *"Lord, I am so sorry but I am getting so sleepy. You see, I am not able to do even the simple task of staying awake to listen to you. How can you expect me to do bigger tasks? Lord, again I am so sorry. Good night, my dear God, and I'll talk to you tomorrow."*

After what I perceived as a long and peaceful sleep, a strong, awakening whisper made me get up in haste.

"What matters most, what matters most, Thalia," the powerful, unwavering voice said.

The voice was too powerful to ignore, and my whole being was terrified. I could still feel the warm whisper in my ear.

I looked toward the altar and suddenly the fear went away. I asked, "Lord, was it you speaking to me? If so, please tell me what you meant with that phrase."

I went back to sleep and woke up with a clear answer in my head:

I should not worry too much about little things as long as I try hard to cling to what matters most in life, which is to love God from the heart. If loving God is my guiding principle in life, I can never go wrong. Good words, good thoughts, and favorable actions will follow. If I do the thing that matters most, I will be motivated to share whatever blessings I receive from Him, and be encouraged to deliver whatever tasks He assigns me to do.

When time abounds, I should use it for God's glory by studying the scriptures so I can share His truth with other people; when basic material needs are met, I should spare some money for the poor instead of creating more wants for myself; when health is in a perfect state, I should remember to visit the ill and pray for them; when love is all around me, I should pass it on to those who need it; when miracles happen, tell it to others so they will see the goodness of God; when life is comfortable, offer little sacrifices by fasting voluntarily, twice a week.

Furthermore, in my journey toward holiness, I fall and stumble into temptation but God will give me the grace to be aware of my sins and recognize the areas where I am weak so I will be stronger when the next challenge comes. Sin alienates me from the purpose that He has set for me, but I should keep on striving to please Him, believing in my heart that God does not look at my spiritual successes but looks at how much I have striven to succeed. There are times when I do not see Him and feel

Him in my pursuits. I should continue to strive, with a firm faith that He will reward me in His time. These are not difficult to do if I do the thing that matters most: to love God from the heart.

I started writing this book a few days after this dream. When the book was close to its completion, Satan came to me in the form of captivating worldly ornaments to lure me to stop writing this book and follow him instead. There were times when he succeeded. Many times, I got distracted by activities that seemed to be more interesting than writing a book. The struggle was hard and endless. Listening to Satan, was easy but offending God was tormenting. Every time I felt like entertaining Satan's cunning ways, I think of that night when I heard warm whispers in my ear that said, "What matters most, what matters most, Thalia."

A Thought

A simple spiritual dream matters a lot to someone who tries to establish a personal relationship with God.

Prayer

My Lord, my Shepherd, my Master, help me to recognize your voice when you call out my name. Make me sensitive to the promptings of my soul if it is for the goodness of my soul and for your greater glory.

TWENTY-TWO

To Nana, I Love You—Gil

JC Narag—As Told by Her Son, Alexius

Gil's mother, Nana, could not send him to college because she was a poor widow. There were six other children to take care of.

But Gil found a way to go to college via a different route—driving a talented young man to school who was in a wheelchair. He was born with legs too weak to walk him around.

Gil waited in the corridors or in any vacant room next to Dan's class. He paid close attention to the lectures and even took down notes. Sometimes he would even repeat some of the high points in a teacher's lecture, or reproduce some jokes or anecdotes.

One instructor or guest lecturer once talked about insurance policies. Gil got interested in the plan.

A fisherman friend who already had an insurance policy later introduced a plan to Gil.

Gil and his ward lived in Manila for a while as the latter tried his luck in the city as an accountant.

When Dan got married, Gil joined a fishermen's group and also applied for an insurance policy. For years, Gil's group was out in the high seas from morning until late in the afternoon, fishing with their two-meter-long steel harpoons. Most of the time, Gil and his friends used compressors so they could go down into the deep. They caught more and bigger fish this way.

Nana had always been warning her son to be ever careful, but the brave young man always had an answer. "Aw, Nana! Ancham madindin pa u vorra." Loosely translated: "Oh, Nana! Even molten lava can be washed ashore." He meant that there was no need to worry. After all, if anything happened, he would always drift ashore, or would turn up somewhere.

Nana sometimes wondered if Gil cared for her or loved her at all. He spent his leisure time hanging around with friends until late at night. Many times, Nana would throw him pieces of advice, but Gil would never seem to listen.

The day came when Gil failed to come home midmorning after a fishing trip that started early the previous evening. A friend was with him.

Two hours after the pair had left for that fishing trip, which was about three kilometers away, the winds suddenly broke loose and the waves became big and dashed against the fishing boat with great fury.

The whole village waited anxiously, and relatives and friends prayed hard for the two friends.

The next day, the body of Gil's friend was recovered. All covered with seaweed, it was found lying in a heap at low tide, among the corals.

There was still no news about Gil. Two more days passed. Inquiries and text messages were exchanged. Especially concerned was my family because Gil's father was my father's cousin, and one of Gil's sisters had lived with my sister and me in Manila for years.

Finally, the sad news came—that Gil was dead. His body was found sandwiched between two giant rocks along the shore.

Nana's lamentation reached the heavens as she uttered Gil's name with a loud cry every time she saw anything that would remind her of her son.

Before the funeral, Gil's Nana wanted to be sure she would not be reminded too much of Gil. He had been such a good son and his mother's heart was torn into bits. So she gathered Gil's belongings to put into a sack to be deposited somewhere. With a heavy heart, she folded neatly each article of clothing—pants, shirts, handkerchiefs, etc.

One small package wrapped in a plastic envelope dropped as she flipped through some papers from a locked drawer that was forced open.

"Darna, this is different. Find out what it is," said Nana.

Darna, Gil's sister, read the contents for Nana. Her face lit up as she told Nana, "This is a life insurance policy for P200,000.00. And Nana, you are the beneficiary. You receive double that amount because of Gil's accidental death."

Clipped in the corner of the insurance policy was a note in Gil's penmanship: "To Nana—I love you.—Gil."

"He never told me anything about this. He had to pay the premiums from his meager earnings because he loved me!" Nana was crying like a child.

A Thought

Love is expressed in many ways. In his lifetime, Gil never had a chance to tell his mother that he loved her. The note clipped in the life insurance policy served as an assurance that he really did.

Prayer

Lord, may we never waste our time on earth by living as if you did not exist, for we do not know when you may call us to eternity.

TWENTY-THREE

The Gift of Sacrificial Love

Thalia Narag Cayetano

Every Christmas since we got married, Kay and I have agreed not to spend money to buy gifts for each other. Instead, we have resolved to buy gifts for the poor kids. Having both come from a Third World country, we know that Christmas can be hard for the less fortunate. This act of love with sacrifice has been our greatest gift to Jesus on His birthday.

It was a day after Thanksgiving in 2003. The first smell of the pine trees prodded us to put up our first Christmas tree in our new house. Every day, we bought and wrapped little, inexpensive gifts for people who have become a part of our lives. As Christmas came closer, the wrapped gifts that were evenly arranged under the tree seemed to look like a big Christmas tree skirt.

Christmas Eve was cold and foggy but the sunlight was struggling to stream down from between the trees. I thought I was the first to get a glimpse of this spectacle, but I was surprised to see my husband sitting pensively in the room where I kept the boxes and some stuff that I had yet to wrap for Christmas.

"I was just wondering…have we bought a gift for Avanina? She is now two years old and I'm sure she now understands that Christmas is about receiving, too. Last night, I forgot to mention to you that she was staring at the gifts under the tree while whispering to me, 'Daddy, open gifts,'" my husband said seriously.

Embarrassed that I forgot to tell him about my plans, I said, "At an early age, I think she should start to understand that giving is more important than receiving. Not giving gifts for each other has ceased to be a sacrifice because it has become our joy as the years go by. I think it's time to start a brand new sacrifice for Jesus by not giving the little one anything this Christmas."

"But she's only two years old. Can't we spare her from our Christmas whims? Well, you're the boss. Whatever you think is best," he said. That's Kay. Agree or disagree, he never argues.

"She already received enough gifts from our friends. Let us just sacrifice not to give her anything," I further suggested.

He nodded his head as a gesture of approval, though I knew what he was thinking: "My wife is in a fantasy land again."

The streets were quiet on Christmas day. Shopping malls and the restaurants were closed. But at noontime, the three of us started to open our hearts for people whose hearts had nowhere to go. Joyfully, we drove to deliver gifts to some of our friends. Our last stop was in a shelter that was being occupied by at least ten families. As we approached the door, we saw the kids' faces lighten up as we delivered clothes, cookies, candies, sodas, and milk. Seeing the children jubilating over the simple presents that we brought was the best gift that we had ever received.

When we got home, the Christmas tree was standing tall without the gifts underneath it. Our daughter was looking at the tree wondering why nothing was left for us to open.

Suddenly, when it was almost time for dinner, a FedEx truck came to deliver three big boxes for our daughter. They were sent by our friends from Canada and Australia. A few minutes later, a friend of ours also came to deliver more gifts for her.

Avanina was reluctant to open them at first. She needed an assurance that they were really for her.

"Open them, baby. They are all for you," her daddy said.

"Wow" was the only word you could hear from her as she noticed that underneath the brown paper package were gift boxes all covered in beautiful Christmas wraps.

With a smile on my face, I looked up and thanked God for giving us a lovely message that real joy comes from giving from the heart. It is a spice added to this joy when receiving something that was heartily given.

A Thought

Giving gifts on Christmas day itself has always given us a personal happiness. We do this so as not to make the recipient obliged to give us gifts in return.

Prayer

O Lord, help us to understand that when true love is expressed, true joy is reaped.

TWENTY-FOUR

Messages in Pink

JC Narag

My clerk Connie, my driver Cesar, and I missed snacks and lunch as I tried to finish a long-overdue commitment: the translation from English to Ivatan of the Novena to the Mother of Perpetual Help. Ivatan is the native language of the people of Batanes, the northernmost province of the Philippines.

The preceding night, all three of us were in the southern communities for an information drive and free movies. We were supposed to just take it easy that day, but Father Gumy Hernandez, the parish priest, said that women devotees of the Blessed Mother had been waiting for a long, long time for the novena's translation.

With a pen and paper, I started translating the novena. The work was non-stop. In our place, offices close for lunch, but at 12:30 p.m. the information office was still open. I told Connie and

Cesar to go home for lunch just before one o'clock.

I had finished the translation but there were parts somewhere in the middle, and near the end, that needed some revisions. The markers were missing, so I began turning and turning the pages. I was also singing softly the closing hymn of the novena, in English and in Ivatan:

Mother of Christ, Mother of Christ
(Ina ni Christo, Ina ni Christo)

What shall I ask of thee
(Ango yahes ko dimo)

I do not sigh for the wealth of earth
(Yahes ko ava u kaynakman)

For the joys that fade and flee
(Kan kayayakan du tana ya)

Mother of Christ, Mother of Christ
(Ina ni Christo, Ina ni Christo)

This do I long to see
(Niaya u yahes ko dimo)

The bliss untold, which thy arms enfold
(Nu kayayakan a yapo du tanoro mo)

The treasure upon thy knee
(Niyaya u uyud ko a ichahoho)

Just then, I became aware of a pink liquid on my right thumb. It rested on the mid portion of my thumb, a little to the right. I thought it was some drippings from the pink stencil eraser from the governor's office on the second floor. So I quickly wiped it off with a tissue.

I continued to sing to myself the second part of the final hymn of the Novena to the Mother of Perpetual Help:

> Mother of Christ, Mother of Christ
> (Ina ni Christo, Ina ni Christo)
>
> This do I ask of thee
> (Niaya u yahes ko dimo)
>
> When the voyage is o'er
> (Du kavusan nu viay)
>
> Oh stand on the shore
> (Vayaten pa yaken)
>
> And show Him at last to me
> (Kapasinchad mo niaken di Hesus)

And I continued flipping the pages to try to locate the portions that needed improvement. As I was singing and turning the pages, there it was again—the pink liquid! This time, it was on my right forefinger, between the bottom and the next joint. I looked at the liquid again and again. It was wet, and the edges, with tiny bubbles, were elevated, as if to prevent the whole thing from dripping.

It was more heart-shaped than it was round or oblong.

When it was about to dry completely, I got a piece of chalk and rolled it over the form. Then I wiped it off clean with a tissue. I also looked for the tissue I'd used earlier and I put all of these together in a little box.

When the janitors and the clerks of the governor's office came back from lunch, I asked them if they were using pink stencil erasers. No, they said. The stencil eraser they were using was blue, not pink. They all helped me to look for any pink drips on the wooden floor, but there were none. Besides, the ceiling in my office was all white, unstained.

I hurried to the residence of Father Gumy to tell him about the pink manifestations. The good father said, "See, the mother of God loves you and she wants to tell you that she is very happy that you have finished the translation of the novena from English to Ivatan."

I went home to tell my husband and my children about the marvelous events. My husband, Nick, provided a cover for the chalk and the tissues that I used to wipe off the pink manifestations. Then he put them in his wallet.

There is a postscript to this story. On June 8, 2004, my son-in-law, Kay, brought me to the Quirino Memorial Medical Center for treatment of an on-and-off headache. My husband was not feeling anything unusual at the time. But Kay insisted that Nick come along for the checkups, especially since his brother, Dr. Karlo, was on duty. Kay said it would give him a good feeling, traveling back to California—if both of us submitted to check-ups.

Dr. Karlo said I could go home that night. I was glad because I could continuously work on my manuscript on the pink forms that had landed on my hands twenty years back. But what was the exact date? Nick's old wallet where the data was kept was at home, and home was about three hours by airplane.

Nick was to stay for observation and more medical examinations, for his blood pressure was unusually high. As he was wheeled away for an ultrasound, he tossed me his wallet for safekeeping. One secret pocket of his wallet was unusually hard and full. I unzipped the pocket and shook it upside-down. One little piece of chalk fell on my lap. I gave the wallet a look-over and I found it had scars all over; it looked ancient and haggard. I carefully brought out the once white, now yellow-with-age tissues. Inside were white, pink-stained chalk pieces and some disintegrated whitish-pinkish tissues. I read the notes on the tissue cover:

"August 8, 1983: Naring (JC Narag) wiped off with these chalk and tissues pink formations on her right thumb, and later, on her right forefinger—after she finished translating from English to Ivatan, the Novena to the Mother of Perpetual Help."

I quickly retrieved every little piece, folded back the tissue wrapper and returned the same in its original slot in my husband's wallet. Then I thanked the Blessed Mother of God and asked her to pray for my husband's health.

All these events that had transpired during our trip to the city explained why Nick suddenly decided to look for his twenty-year-old wallet and take it with him to Manila.

A Thought

Total obedience was the example set by the Blessed Mother as she accepted God's will to be the mother of our Savior. Through the pink manifestations, she showed me her love and approval when I accepted without hesitation the priest's request to translate the novena.

Prayer

Lord, when I hear you calling in the night or even in the midst of a busy day, may I learn to pay attention and move in haste to do the task that you assign me to do.

TWENTY-FIVE

Chula's Dinner

Thalia Narag Cayetano

The afternoon sun was quickly followed by the gleaming twilight. It was only the blurry vision that stopped me and my brother Demy from continuing to play badminton. We sat on the bench in our front yard, welcoming into our nostrils the most refreshing air of the day. *What more can I ask for at this moment?* I thought. In a few minutes, mother would be calling us for dinner. I knew that it was going to be another festive dinner with each member of the family sharing some fascinating stories to fill the house with merriment.

The gate bell rang and it was a little boy selling fish. I peeked into the basket that was half-open. The little boy seemed hopeful that we were going to buy some of his fish. Ever since we were kids, Mom would never let a vendor leave empty-handed. Out of compassion, she would buy fish, vegetables, and all sorts of different things even if she'd just bought the same from other vendors who had come earlier.

Chula, one of the town folks, stopped walking to take a glimpse of the fish. She looked pale and haggard. Like a three-second movie, I envisioned her and her husband and their twelve children sitting around an empty table, all hungry and thin from malnutrition. Chula earned a living by giving a hand to families who needed temporary help in their homes and farms.

"Chula, here's your bag. Allow me and my brother to take care of your food tonight. Pick any fish of your choice. Make sure it is enough for your family's dinner," I whispered to her as I handed her an empty bag.

Shyly but gladly, Chula said, "How come you were able to read my mind? While I was walking home, my heart was tearing apart, knowing that I have nothing to feed my family tonight. Thank you very much."

I heard mom's voice calling for dinner. My brother and I quickly ran inside.

"Enjoy your dinner, Chula!" Demy said.

Once again, the whole family was sitting around a mirthful table. Demy and I were not particularly jubilant over the good food in front of us. We were silently delighted with the thought that at that moment, another family was enjoying a decent meal.

A Thought

God wants all His children to care for one another.

Prayer

Lord, may I learn not to be confined in my own yard of contentment, but to look beyond my comfort zone to listen to the unspoken needs of my fellow men.

TWENTY-SIX

Saved by the Medals

JC Narag

A tiny bundle was floating before the eyes of survivors of a shipwreck. Still dazed from the traumatic experience, survivors recounted later that many of them just shoved the little bundle toward shore. Many were not even sure the bundle was a baby.

That was Ellen, my sister Kakai's one-year-old baby. Ellen and her parents, who were both grade-school teachers, were crossing the channel from their island town, Sabtang. They were on their way to the capital town of Basco for the provincial athletic meet.

At the port of Ivana, which is the connecting point between Sabtang and any other part of the province, the wooden boat was smashed by strong waves, ejecting all of its passengers.

Ellen's mother carried her baby in a native carriage called an aban, a square sheet with two corners knotted together to form a triangle. The knotted ends locked in the baby's legs and bottom. The other two corners were brought together and strapped over Kakai's right shoulder, secured also in a knot.

But Ellen surely slipped from the carriage and floated away.

Father Gumy Hernandez, parish priest of Ivana, recalled that he saw Kakai in the shallow waters, walking toward the ill-fated banca. Slung on her shoulders was a white, empty sheet that he said could have been the baby's carriage.

"She was already on the shore. A little while longer and I could not see her anymore from my telescope. I know Kakai; she would have darted back through the waves to look for her baby and her husband," the priest said.

Late in the afternoon, twelve bodies were recovered and brought to the local hospital. One of these was Kakai's, and another was that of her husband.

Ellen fought bravely for her life. At several points, my family and I thought she was going to die. But the doctors, nurses, attendants, and other workers went out of their way to save the child. My nurse cousin Amada volunteered her services for twenty-four hours at the hospital even though she was on vacation. Many friends sought divine assistance for Ellen. I prayed constantly, together with Lin, my sister, for the agonizing baby.

As my sister Kakai's body lay with the other victims at the local hospital, I looked all over her dripping clothes for any religious relics that could be hidden somewhere. I did not find the rosary I gave her. Her pockets were empty. There were no medals, or anything on her husband's clothes.

Then I inspected Ellen's shirts and baby dresses. Securely pinned on the breast of Ellen's dress were three gold-plated miraculous medals of the Blessed Mother of God. All three medals had their own safety pins attached to a much bigger one, pinned on Ellen's dress.

Those who witnessed or heard of this ill-fated event provided Ellen a special place in their hearts. She grew up under the care of one of my sisters. Ellen is now married with two sons. She has no memory of her parents, but she knows in her heart that her mother's love was as vast as the ocean.

A Thought

Kakai's love was enormous. Undaunted by the furious ridges of water, she rushed back to look for her husband and her child.

Prayer

Lord, may all husbands appreciate the love of their wives; may all children see with love their mothers' sacrifices; and may all wives and mothers learn to endure the challenges of preserving the family, with the knowledge that their real reward awaits them in heaven if only they put their hope and trust in you. Amen.

Twenty-seven

A Mending Criticism

Thalia Narag Cayetano

My first day in a marketing firm, on September 15, 1994, was the most unforgettable among all my first days in any job that I landed.

My heart was captured by Annie, a young lady who tried to befriend me as soon as I got myself settled in my cubicle. Every morning, she would get me into an interesting conversation. Some parts of her stories would always hang in the air unless I met with her for lunch to pick up the missing pieces. We became close too soon; I felt like we never passed through the nodding-acquaintance stage. On weekends, we would also spend some time together to either see a movie or chat over a cup of coffee.

Before long, she became comfortable talking to me about anything, even using foul words to describe people we both knew at work. She was destroying people's reputations, and the worst part was I did not have the nerve to stop her!

Another co-worker warned me that to be seen with her all the time would surely bedevil me, for almost everyone at work knew who the real Annie was. That worried me, because as a new employee I wanted to be known for who I was and not for whom I was with.

Many times, I came home distressed. Before long, I started to avoid Annie. She did not have the slightest idea that behind those premeditated excuses of not being able to go with her was my plan of breaking away from her friendship. But breaking up with a girlfriend was not as easy as I thought. Despite my cold signs, she kept coming to me to tell her abominable stories.

After a few sleepless nights, I started to muster all my bravery to tell Annie that I wanted our friendship to end.

"Annie, I want to talk to you about something that other people may not have the courage to talk to you about. Are you aware that every time you destroy the reputation of another, you are ruining your own? I used to admire and like you, but it saddens me that you have changed. It definitely annoys me when you start gossiping about people that we both know. It is getting unconscionable and hard to tolerate."

With eyes big in wonder, Annie replied, "But I am what I am. I thought you accepted me for who I am."

In a soft but assured voice I said, "You are what you are; that's why I cannot take it anymore.

Yours is a personality problem, and it's hard to change that. Today, I am telling you that I am no longer interested in anything that has to do with you. Our friendship has to end right here and now. Maybe our relationship cannot transcend the coworker level. I cannot be untrue to you anymore by pretending that I still want your friendship if I do not."

I tried to be calm amid a hidden anger. My only objective was to tell her why I wanted to sever my ties with her, and then stop seeing her.

"That's it? You came to me to say that our friendship is over? I can't believe that you did not ask me to mend my ways first. Your words seem final and condemning. You think you are righteous, with very strict morals. But if I may be honest with you, I find you to be too unforgiving by saying that you want to end our friendship right here and now. Well, if that is what you want, fine with me. Our friendship will not last if you are that theatrical and unreasonably puritanical, anyway," Annie said with agitation.

For a few minutes, it was not the painful exchange of words but the spellbinding silence that estranged us from each other. After a while, I heard Annie say "sorry" in between sobs. Listening to her mumble disconnected phrases gave me a painful blow in the chest.

Yes, she is right. I am too unforgiving. I think of myself as the righteous one when I see a person in error. Why don't I look at myself first? Why don't I realize that I myself am sinful and not perfect?

Still in tears, Annie continued, "I am so embarrassed, but thank you for pointing out my faults. You are the first one who has ever talked to me about my errors. My parents were never around to guide me when I was young. My grandmother passed away a few years after she decided to take care of me. I guess I am such an angry person. There is so much bitterness in my heart. I have had a lot of friends but nobody was hardly ever there for me. Somehow, I knew deep inside that one day I would lose your beautiful friendship, too. What makes you different from my other friends was that you cared enough to tell me my flaws before deciding to leave me. If you ever change your mind, I still want to be your friend. I promise to watch my mouth from this moment on. If ever we can be close friends again, I would expect you to continue being honest with me."

Annie's humble and apologetic statement touched and humbled me. In one second, I felt God's humongous love twining its way into my heart, wanting to replace the tiny love that had been residing in there. Talking to myself, I said: *Is Annie the difficult person or am I? Where is the love in my heart? Is it too small to bring about patience and understanding?*

"Annie," I said softly as I put my hand on her shoulder, "I am so sorry, too. For some reason, the bitterness built up inside me until it was too hard for me to forgive you. I did not know that it only takes openness to get our friendship going. Right here and now, I forgive you. Please forgive me, too. Let us not treat this day as the final day, but as a new beginning of a lasting friendship. Today, I promise you that I'll be more open, forgiving, and understanding."

With a smile I continued, "Okay, how about this? Let us agree not to criticize other people but to criticize each other instead. When you see me doing something not right, you call my attention to it right away and I'll do the same for you. The one who is too proud to take criticism shall spend money for our lunch."

"It's a deal," Annie said as she put her arms around me.

Annie and I became the greatest critics, not of other people but of ourselves. We started talking about family relationships, morality, God, and spirituality. Our friendship grew as we continued to handle with acceptance and humility one of the most fault-finding and pride-hurting words in any relationship: criticism.

A Thought

I was so self-righteous that I failed to acknowledge my own frailties. Annie's admission of her fault moved my heart to forgive.

Prayer

Lord, may I learn to attune my heart with yours so I may love, understand, and forgive like you do.

TWENTY-EIGHT

Mysteries Under the Jamaican Tree

JC Narag

About six weeks before Thalia, my sixth child, left for California to join her husband, she had a dream. The Blessed Mother of God wanted a grotto with her statuette under the tree in our front yard. The dream came back again and again.

Every afternoon for over a week, my family and Thalia's close friend at work would gather limestone for the grotto.

When my two youngest children and I were in the city, we visited the stores selling religious items. We would comb the shops and fan out for the choicest statuette. When we finally selected one, each of us led one another to the statue that was a common choice. Thalia was filled with wonder when she saw the statue of the Blessed

Mother. "That's exactly how she looked like in my dreams," she said.

After the grotto had been blessed by the parish priest, some mysterious events began to take place here.

The Lamp That Kept Burning

There was a little kerosene lamp that I kept lighted night and day for the Blessed Mother of God. The metal fuel container burned gas fast. So every morning, I tried to replenish the kerosene. But each time I opened the fuel container and dipped my forefinger into it, the tank was half full. It was only on the seventh day that the lamp ran out of fuel.

I had been using the little lamp for more than thirty years. It lighted up the mini altar in the bedroom day and night. Its fuel lasted only for twenty-four hours, not for six days.

On the seventh day, I looked at the face of the Blessed Mother long and hard. I asked her to continue to be ever-present in our lives, to watch over us and pray for us so that God would be the center of our lives. I told myself that perhaps the Blessed Mother Mary was truly sympathetic to us for the perpetual increases in the price of oil— which triggers untold miseries for us all.

The Roses Would Not Die, But Why?

Near the lamp was a cute flower vase for the Blessed Mother. That first day, after the blessings,

I put some freshly cut roses in the vase, plus a few vines of cadena de amor with abundant pink flowers twining on tiny driftwood. For the living room, I prepared a similar set of blooms—freshly cut red roses and pink cadena de amor climbing on rare twigs.

The next day, the roses and cadena de amor in the living room had withered and some petals had fallen on the floor.

But the roses and cadena de amor for the Blessed Mother in the grotto stayed on for five days. On the seventh day, the petals of the cadena de amor became much lighter and some fell off from the stems. The roses faded, too, and just disappeared. Whether they were blown by the wind or someone took them away, I will never know. But they were kept fresh and beautiful by an unseen hand—for about five days.

Saved in a Flood

About two o'clock in the afternoon of February 22, 2000, my youngest daughter, Ava, was relishing a late lunch and I was reading *Tea Time for Women* when I heard an unusual sound.

The flood control system near the house was alive with the rumbling sound of stones and rocks rolling and tumbling over one another as they were carried downward by a flash flood.

In town, the rainfall had been light the night before and that morning. Unknown to the townsfolk, however, was that the rain had been unusually heavy throughout the hills and farms in the surrounding area.

Watching the direction of the floodwaters made me nervous. The canal was filled with water rushing westward in the direction of the district houses. That meant that there were obstructions along the waterways. In about thirty minutes, the flood would come rushing into our front yard and possibly into the house.

I bundled up my seven-month-old grandson and gave instructions that he be brought to my cousin's place about half a kilometer away. Then I waited for my husband and two sons, plus Charlotte, a grade-school student in my care, to come home. We were to proceed to my cousin's place, away from the flood.

The house helper was putting away to safety some precious things. Me, I thought nothing was more precious than life, so I was not concerned about my orchids or anything else.

But before leaving the house, I prayed before the statue of our Lady of Fatima. I asked her to take care of everyone, and everything she considered important. The floodwaters had not reached the front yard yet.

Charlotte came running home, soaked to the bones. "Don't take anything else with you! We are leaving for Vasay, where we will be safe from the flood!" I screamed.

"Please, may I get a coat and one—"

"Okay, just get one dress. You don't have time to choose. We are leaving now," I answered.

The water was above our knees all along the streets to my cousin Oscar's house. The current was so strong it washed away cooking tanks and other merchandise, which we had to dodge on our way to safety.

My cousin, a judge, did not ask us any questions. He and his wife, Mila, also my cousin, just took us in and prepared a feast for us "refugees."

Ava and Demy, my youngest two children, between gulps of hot soup at Oscar's place, recounted how terrible the flood was. Dem had not been aware of the flood and he said he was whistling a merry tune as he left his office that afternoon. But when he reached the bridge near our house, he was surprised to see that the water had already surged into the front yard, then to the house. He saw Ava and some friends, trying to get some valuables to safety. Big Max was also there, trying to catch the washing machine that was floating a few feet from the door.

When the rain ceased and the floods stopped gushing, we all came home to see the house in a most heartbreaking state. The mud was an inch deep in the living room and about four inches outside. The flood left a dark marking to show that the water went as high as the piano.

Six months before, there had been an intensity-seven earthquake that knocked down and uprooted giant trees. These could have been carried and deposited along the flood control system.

An army of young men and women and some elderly folks soon came to the house to offer material, spiritual, and all kinds of assistance.

Some came to wash blankets, to shovel mud from the path, or even just to cook and socialize and be merry after a bout with that flash flood. Neighbors and friends who lived in houses farther away from the flood came to help. Even Philip, whose house was in the direction of the flood, and who fought the flood to help put things up on our rooftop, came again to help.

The crowd that gathered for two days did not fail to notice a minor miracle under the Jamaican tree—the grotto of our Lady of Fatima and its immediate surroundings, including all the plants and ornamentals there, and the man-made mini mountain were spared from the wrath of the flash flood.

One vanda bloom, located close to the grotto, shot up proudly for almost a week afterwards. The bonsai (balete, native tea, aryes, etc.) and the miniature forest were unscathed. They suffered no dislocations, or bruises, or scars.

Most important of all, none of us got hurt. Even little Beedoy was okay and went on entertaining us with his never-ending baby antics.

Nothing of much importance was lost, except one little antique jar, and some plastic houseware items.

A Thought

The Blessed Mother of God, in answer to my prayer, took care of everything that she considered important. No doubt, my family's earthly lives were important to her, too.

147

Prayer

Lord, help me to love the Blessed Mother and trust her intercessions.

TWENTY-NINE

What Language Do You Speak?

Thalia Narag Cayetano

Coming to the United States of America for the first time was particularly challenging. Aside from the general culture shock, the American accent was almost always hard to grasp.

As soon as I received my authorization to work, I started to religiously look through the papers for job listings. My joy was overwhelming when a placement agency took me in.

In all the companies that I worked for, there always was one common impression that people had of me. They thought of me as a quiet person whose words had to be bought for a high price. Aside from being naturally quiet, the language barrier prevented me from talking too much, until I became comfortable with my own silence. In the quiet of my heart, I found it easier to get acquainted with God even at work.

After gaining professional experience from my temporary assignments, I decided to accept a permanent position.

One quiet morning, a pretty young lady silently approached my supervisor and asked her, pointing at me, "I heard that she is deaf and mute. Where did she come from?"

With a chuckle, I looked at her and said, "No, I'm not deaf and mute. I'm just quiet, that's all."

Looking extremely embarrassed, the lady gasped, "Oh, I am so sorry. I just overheard somebody saying that about you. I believed it because I haven't heard you talk, either."

I said, "Oh, no. Don't ever feel bad that you said that. I understand that people would think of me as such because of my being unusually quiet."

Overhearing the lady's initial reaction, another lady from behind a partition stood up and asked, "Oh, I finally heard your voice. What language do you speak?"

I answered with a smile, "I speak the language of God, which is love. My mouth is shut almost all the time, but my heart speaks a lot."

The two ladies did not seem to understand my words at that time, but they became my close friends from that day on. Every day, we would have lunch together. We accepted the differences that we had in ethnicity and personality.

One day, while the three of us were having lunch, Katie looked at me and said, "We want to learn the language of God, too. Can you tell us what to do?"

Thrilled that she asked something that I was eager to answer, I said: "Begin by visiting a Christian bookstore. Read the Bible and other inspirational books and start getting involved in your church. It is only by having the knowledge of Jesus's teachings that you can be motivated to love and follow Him. Accept God in your hearts and put Him first in everything that you do. Try to spend some time with your loved ones, too. Listen to their stories and learn to appreciate all the lovely things about them. It will be easier for you to love other people if you love your families first. Before you know it, the love in your heart will have grown, causing you to naturally speak the language of God."

As the days went by, the three of us began to understand one another, even in silence. We came to believe that silence can be a form of speech if one speaks the language of God, which is love.

A Thought

After this unforgettable experience, I started to get the courage to talk more. I learned that my language can bring people to God if it is spoken and demonstrated at the same time.

Prayer

Lord, may I yearn to learn your language and persuade others to speak the same. Help me not to be ashamed of professing my faith in you so you will not be ashamed of me before your Father in heaven.

THIRTY

Walking with Michael

Thalia Narag Cayetano

Michael was eighty-one years old but he said he felt like a child in the presence of God. He was a World War II veteran whose actions and words clearly served as a verification of his faith.

His face was ridged by age lines but his high spirits made him look young. His eyes looked old and weary but they peacefully served as the windows of his soul. His voice was weak and low but his words depicted wisdom and ardor. His self-assured posture always made me envision a young soldier who commanded respect and demanded attention in his prime.

"Do you walk to church every day?" Mike asked softly with a smile.

"Yes, as exercise. How about you, sir? I see you in church every day. Do you live around here?"

"No, I live a few miles from the church, but I walk every day to fulfill a vow. All these years,

God has blessed me with good health, while others are ailing due to old age. My walking daily to church as a sacrifice is my way of expressing my gratitude. I have promised myself to continue doing this until such a time when old age makes me too frail to reach the temple."

After an exchange of introductions, we went on walking and talking as if we had known each other for years.

Because we used the same route, Michael and I would often chance upon each other on our way to the church. After the church service, we intentionally strolled back home together.

While we walked on the side streets, he would tell me of his painful experiences during World War II, when Japanese soldiers tortured Filipino soldiers or civilians who served the American government. Sometimes he would hold my hands as he got into a heartrending part of his story. Often, our walk-time was not sufficient to let us finish a story. And so we would stop at the nearest fast-food restaurant for breakfast or just simply spend a few hours in the house to chat.

Michael would always burst into tears whenever he recounted his experience after the American-Filipino troops retreated to Bataan.

"After the American-Filipino troops surrendered, the Japanese compelled us at gunpoint to leave our fortress in Bataan to march to Pampanga. Many of us suffered from malaria and malnutrition. This suffering was worse than the wounds inflicted by enemy bullets.

"We were made to walk in heavy chains, barefoot under the scorching heat of the sun. Those who were too weak to get up and walk were shot down. Thalia, I saw many of my comrades dropping dead due to physical and emotional torture. Many times, it was my heavy heart that made me want to stop walking. How I wish…how I wish I was able to stop even just to shed a tear for each of them who died during the march," Michael cried.

"Keep crying, Michael. Cry for your comrades in the war. Nobody can stop you from crying," I assured him, while I reached for his hand to comfort him.

After he wiped the last dregs of tears running down his face, Michael gave me a pale, lonely grin.

"Thank you for taking time to listen. You are the first one who has ever taken time to listen to my grief, so many years after the war. I lost my wife a long time ago, and my three children, who now have lives of their own, live far away from me.

My daily walk with Michael became an emotional as well as a moral duty. As the days went by, I started to see his face beam with joy. His walking pace became faster and his speech louder and clearer.

This continued on for months until I had to go to my home town to start a new job. Distance did not stop us from communicating. When I heard the mailman coming, my heart would leap for joy, hoping that I would get a letter from Michael.

Whenever I was in the city for a business trip, I always tried to include him in my busy schedule.

In July 1998, a few days before I left for the United States, we had our last breakfast together. He cupped his hands above my head and said an unusually long prayer. After praying, he looked at me and said, "Thalia, I cannot continue walking with you, but keep going. Do not leave your faith here. Bring it with you. Be a Cursillista wherever you go. Walk with God in faith and you will not stumble even in the dark."

To this day, Michael's words and prayers have become the litanies of my soul. When my faith falters, I think of how he thrived to remain in God's friendship until he was almost done with his life.

A Thought

Every step that I took with Michael was a stride toward my bigger commitment to follow Jesus.

Prayer

Lord, as I enjoy walking alone with you, may I not forget to stop awhile and listen to the wisdom and stories of older Christians who have trodden the road that I am just about to take. May my spirit remain strong even when my body weakens.

THIRTY-ONE

Where Your Joy Must Come From

Thalia Narag Cayetano

Leaving my home town for good to join my husband in the United States was one of the most difficult steps that I ever had to take. My mom for the last time reminded me to continue to be a blessing to the people around me. Pointing to my heart, she said, "All that your heart contains now, you're going to bring them with you to where you are going. God's love and our love joined together will put a smile on your face. Due to geographical distance, your father and I or your brothers and sisters will not be readily available to cry with you or to laugh with you whenever you need us. Do not forget that even without somebody physically around you to share your good and bad moments, think of God and think of us and your day will be blessed."

Is my going to America such a big deal that I have to worry about these things?

My mom was right. For someone like me who grew up in a humble place, living in America could be an enormous challenge to deal with. In this country, where freedom and materialism give easy access to temptation, I knew that I needed to be strong and brave to defend my moral convictions.

My first months in America were full of colorful excitements. Almost everything around me was new. I was amazed to easily find the material things that matched my childhood fantasies, but not for long. Soon, I passed the astonishment stage. I started to look for people who matched my spiritual and emotional whims. It was then that I started to miss my parents, my brothers and sisters, and my Christian friends back home. When I thought of home too much, I could die of loneliness. One day at work, I literally broke down in tears while whispering to myself, "My dear homeland, you are the only haven for my simple and quiet soul. Why did I have to leave you?"

One night, as I cleaned out an old purse, I came across the Prayer of St. Francis of Assisi, written on a small bookmark. I shed tears as I read it. As if my heart taught me a beautiful prayer:

Lord, make me a channel of Thy peace.
Where there is hatred let me sow love.
Where there is injury, pardon.
Where there is doubt, faith.
Where there is despair, hope.
Where there is darkness, light.

Where there is sadness, joy.
O Divine Master, grant that I may not
so much seek to be consoled as to console;
to be understood as to understand;
to be loved as to love.
For it is in giving that we receive.
It is in pardoning that we are pardoned.
It is in dying to self that we are born to eternal life.

Years passed and I got used to not meeting people who were just like my family. I knew that good people were all around me, but my limited community life made it hard to find them.

One day, I met Relan, a godly and prayerful person who reminded me of my family back home. I easily entrusted to him my words and feelings, even my deepest thoughts about God. When I had emotional concerns, I looked for him and there he was, ready to open not only his ears but his heart to listen. I felt like he was my brother who came to unleash all the imprisoned thoughts that I have had since I left my loved ones in my home town. Once again, I felt how good it was to be listened to.

One melancholic summer day, I was feeling down. My husband was away on a trip. Something deeply personal was bothering me. I looked for Relan and I learned that he was also away on a family trip. In deep silence, I closed my eyes and asked God to cheer me up. Instantly, I heard God saying,

"Thalia, you have become so used to being listened to. For the past few months, you have been looking for peo-

ple to understand you and to console you. That is not what I have been asking you to do, remember? Your job is to listen, understand, and console. I allowed you to meet Relan to remind you once again how good it feels to have someone to listen to your joys and sorrows so you will be more motivated to do the same.

Open your heart to people. Answer your phone when it rings, get the door when the doorbell chimes, and you will know that there are a lot of people who have greater needs than you do. Many of them need somebody like you who has the time to listen to their cries. Go now. I am sending you on a mission. Make my love known to some-one who has never loved or who has never been loved before. Make me seen where I am not found. That is where your joy must come from."

I opened my eyes and I saw again a copy of the Prayer of St. Francis of Assisi pinned against the wall in my cubicle.

After a few seconds, my cell phone rang and it was Lori, asking me to meet her after work so she could finally disclose a secret that she had been keeping from her family for more than eight years.

When I got home, I got a message from Gail that she was coming over to the house to talk to me about something deeply personal that she was not at liberty to tell anyone but me.

Before I went to bed, I had a long conversation with God. I thanked Him for teaching me even in silence and for trusting me to work with Him on a mission.

From that day on, I have tried to make myself available to anyone who needs to talk to me. My husband gives me his full consent to dedicate any extra time that I have to share God's love with those who need it. On weekends, I do not want to waste my time. I strive to finish my house chores so I can spend quality time with my husband and my daughter. Otherwise, my time spent with a friend has no quality at all.

My friend Relan has continued to be my confidant and my trusted guide in my walk with Jesus. My conscience dictates that I should try to fight the temptation of wanting to talk to him all the time. Whenever I miss my family back home, I open my heart to those who are hurt and lonely. This is where my joy comes from.

A Thought

I kept looking for the things that I was missing and I failed to appreciate the things that I already had. God spoke to me in silence, making me aware that I can use my loneliness as an opportunity to grow in love and in faith.

Prayer

Lord, let my every prayer be a holy conversation with you. May I learn to listen to you just as I want to be listened to.

THIRTY-TWO

I Saw Mommy Weeping for Santa Claus

Thalia Narag Cayetano

It was Christmas Eve again. My wish list for Santa was long. I was six years old and I knew exactly what I wanted. With my heart full of gladness, I slipped my wish list in one of the three big stockings hanging by the window in the little girls' bedroom.

Verna, my second to the eldest sister, was using Santa as a reason for everything that she wanted us, the three youngest in the family, to do.

"At exactly three o'clock this afternoon, I want you, Thalia, Ava, and Demy to take a nap. Otherwise, Santa will take your names out from his list. He does not give gifts to disobedient children."

I was six, Ava four, and Demy three. We did whatever Verna ordered us to do for fear that

Santa would not come to put gifts in our stockings.

That particular Christmas day, I woke up seeing the stockings empty. Verna said that Santa did not come because my eyes were open when it was time for him to fill the stockings.

How could Santa have known that I was pretending to be asleep that night?

I was already six years old and I was too old for Santa stories, but the truth is, I still believed that the real Santa came out of nowhere to give gifts to children. That year, I was getting curious to see how Santa looked in person.

Demy and Ava cried when they saw the empty stockings.

"No, he is coming tonight to deliver the gifts personally. Don't you want to see him in person?" Verna said with glee.

"I thought he didn't want to show his face; that's why he didn't come when I was awake last night," I said.

"Well, he changed his mind. He wanted you guys to see him this time."

Maybe I was so excited to see him that I did not question how come Santa changed his mind the moment my youngest brother and sister started to cry. Actually, I should have wondered how he was able to communicate to my big sister right at that moment.

The night was dazzling with Christmas lights but the rain was falling heavily, producing melodies as they dropped on some cans for recycling at the back door.

At seven that evening, a red and white form started to appear by the low-rise gate, which had been left open. With a cute stride, he walked into the front yard, almost dancing.

"Here is Santa Claus!" I yelled.

All of us ran to the porch. Since the grass was slippery from the heavy rains, Santa slid to the ground on his back. He immediately got up and danced as if it was a part of his choreography. The three of us kids laughed as we saw this happen. He fell three more times, and every time this happened we just burst into laughter.

He came closer to the porch and started to push some small gifts into the hollow-designs of the deck. I looked at him in awe as I noticed the gifts wrapped with our names written on them. In a subdued voice, he said "Merry Christmas" twice or thrice and then he waved his hand goodbye while walking away.

For the last time, before he reached the gate, Santa stumbled, with his knees and elbows hitting hard against the cement pathway. This time, it was obvious that it was not a part of his dance step, for it took some time before he could get up again. My mom prepared to run to him, but before she could reach him, he ran away very quickly.

The three of us opened our gifts. Suddenly, I remembered what I was missing. He forgot to give me a bicycle! That was the first thing on my list. I ran to my mom to ask her how Santa could have forgotten something, but I saw her shedding tears as she looked in the direction of the gate.

She said, "Maybe his boots were too big for him, that's why he tripped several times."

My heart was torn apart as I saw my mom really concerned for Santa.

Three more hours had passed and I overheard my mom having a conversation with my dad in their bedroom.

"Let me see your elbows. How about your knees? Did you slide again after you left the house?" my mom asked.

"Yes, I stumbled really bad before I reached Naty's place," my dad replied.

"Oh," he continued, "did Thalia ask for her bicycle? I looked in all the stores but I couldn't find any. It was too late to order one from the city."

I tried to suppress my tears by closing my eyes. It was hard to believe that the Santa who fell to the ground several times that cold and rainy night was my father. Quietly, I walked out from the little girls' bedroom, which was just across from my parents'.

Were my parents actually spending money for all those gifts? What if my father was able to find a bicycle from the store? Could he afford to buy one? Did I just not hear from my mom that they were trying to save money for my oldest sister's college education?

Soon, my parents came out to the living room. My father was wearing a long-sleeved shirt and long pants. His hair was wet and he was smiling.

Trying to pretend that I had not heard their conversation, I looked at him and said, "I am so happy about my gifts from Santa. Seeing him in person was more than anything else in this world to me."

For the first time, I gave my father a long and loving look. After a tight embrace, I silently promised myself that next Christmas, I would not hang my stocking and be quiet about my amusing discovery.

That Christmas and onward, my younger sister and brother need not hang stockings for Christmas because Santa came to the house to personally deliver gifts. He also went from house to house giving gifts to other children in the neighborhood.

When Demy and Ava were old enough to know the truth about their family Santa, they too decided to stop requesting gifts from him. Together with our older siblings, the three of us joined our parents and their friends to sing carols anonymously to less fortunate families, and hand them gifts after singing.

A Thought

Anyone who heard this story thought that I was too old to believe in Santa at six years. But what I know is that believing in Santa was one of the highlights of my childhood. My father's inspiring example of generosity and sacrifice touched my heart as a child.

Prayer

Lord, let all the children in the world discover the marvelous love their parents have for them. And may all parents try to reach out to their neighbors and extend to them their simple joys.

THIRTY-THREE

Unfailing Love

Thalia Narag Cayetano

Alex was a young boy when he saw an old woman counting the coins she had kept in a knotted handkerchief.

"Lola, what are you doing?" asked Alex.

"Counting the money I saved to pay for a lawyer."

"Is your money enough to pay him? Can't other people help you aside from a lawyer? I know a lot of helpful people who can give their services for free," he said.

"Well, young boy, only a lawyer can help me straighten out a dispute over a land property. I heard that lawyers' fees cost a fortune. I don't know yet how much he is going to ask," she responded with an anxious smile.

That afternoon, Alex came home with a very pensive look.

"Mom, do lawyers help a lot of people? Can I be a lawyer when I get old so I can help the people,

167

especially those who don't have money to pay for their lawyers?" Alex asked with a serious look on his face.

"You don't have to be a lawyer to be able to help. But, yes, lawyers have the opportunity to help people. To be a lawyer, you need to go to a law school in the city and pass the bar exam," Mom replied.

Alex was compassionate even as a little boy. Mom and his teachers said that at the age of seven, although one of the naughtiest boys in school, his level of maturity was highly admirable. He was always referred to as the small but tough defender because in school and in the community he fought particularly for the weak, the abused, and the disadvantaged. He was never afraid to fight, even if his opponents were bigger and older.

Alex recounted how the old woman he saw counting coins out of a hankie kindled his desire to become a lawyer. His interest was further aroused when martial law began and he heard stories about the abuses of the strong and mighty, including lawyers. He later told Mom that several times he eavesdropped when she and Dad talked about the harm that was done to the poor across the country.

When it was time for Alex to leave for the city to take up law, Mom reminded him, "Son, don't forget that helping the poor when you become a lawyer is your commitment not only to us, but also to God. Remember that the poor are very special to God."

Alex started his pre-law studies in his home town and transferred to the city to finish all the way to law school. Right after he took the bar exam in

1995, Alex came home to his birthplace. That day, when the result of the bar was released, he was on one of the far islands helping his uncle with his political campaign for congress.

The heat of the noontime sun was penetrating through his skin when he heard on the radio that he'd made it through the bar exams. Quietly, Alex left the crowd and walked straight away until he felt he was alone. He sat in solitude under a tree and clasped his hands in prayer:

"Lord, I thank you for allowing me to pass the bar exam. You know the reason why I wanted to become a lawyer. As I promised, I will be particularly kind and helpful to the poor."

Soon, Alex left for the city to work as one of the lawyers at the Land Registration Authority. After a few months, he accepted an offer to work as a defense attorney in one of the prestigious law firms in the city. He gained popularity as bystanders watched him perform in court. Soon, people looking for representation would choose him as their lawyer.

I shed tears in admiration every time Alex recounts how he managed to maintain his dignity while working for a reputable firm. Because all his clients were wealthy, many times, he would receive a huge envelope of cash, either as a bribe or as a personal appreciation of his good work, but he would not accept it. Because he would reject these monetary gifts, some of his clients would secretly put the hulking envelope of cash in his drawer when he was not around. If it was not possible for him to return the money, he would distribute the cash among his staff or have his secretary keep the money to buy snacks for everybody whenever necessary.

As he was earning a good name for the company, the owner of the firm started to plan to affix Alex's name to the business as his partner. Along with this offer was his re-classification to a higher level. While the promotion was lucrative for Alex, his conscience was telling him that God made him a lawyer to be a defender of the poor and not the rich.

It was to everyone's surprise when Alex finally made his decision. He was to leave the prestigious law firm in the city to work for the government as a public attorney in one of the rural areas in the Philippines.

"Why would you want to leave?" Alex's boss asked. "No lawyer has ever left this place except those who I ask to leave. I will make you a millionaire in less than a year. You will never get rich if you work in the government as a public attorney."

"I do realize that sir, but this is my commitment to God. To guard the poor from the cunning ways of the rich and the powerful," Alex said humbly.

"Can you not work here once or twice a week? Can you not..." Alex's boss turned his face away, his eyes red with heavy emotions.

"Working in this company gives me the opportunity to help a lot of people, but it is obvious that the majority of our clients here are rich," he said. "These people can easily find lawyers to defend them, but the poor ones—they need lawyers who are willing to give them legal services even without their money."

With unfailing love burning in his heart for the poor, Alex started to dedicate his life to helping the less fortunate. He made the poor people feel that justice was at their fingertips.

Years later, he decided to come back to his home town to serve as the public attorney in the freshly opened Public Attorney's Office. Today, Alex is the provincial prosecutor of Batanes, but he does not mind working outside his job description. Even after work hours, he generously shares his time with anyone who needs legal advice. Alex's passionate advice and overall disposition inspire opposing parties to iron out conflicts before resorting to the legal method. Some of the disputes get settled even before coming to court.

When asked if it's hard to combine love with law, he answers with a calm smile, "I always think that behind every human law is the divine law. Love is an important component of the divine law. It is not necessary for me to take away passion from my reasoning to be an effective lawyer, for it was love that prodded me to become a lawyer in the first place."

A Thought

The greatest goal in life is that which is focused on God, who sets the real goals for us.

Prayer

Lord, may you be my dream, my goal, my ambition. May you be the driving force in every action that I take. I know that I will never go wrong with you behind me.

LaVergne, TN USA
11 November 2009
163801LV00001B/111/A